Start Your Own

PERSONAL CONCIERGE SERVICE

Additional titles in *Entrepreneur's **Startup Series***

Start Your Own

Bed & Breakfast

Business on eBay

Business Support Service

Car Wash

Child Care Service

Cleaning Service

Clothing Store

Coin-Operated Laundry

Consulting

Crafts Business

e-Business

e-Learning Business

Event Planning Business

Executive Recruiting Service

Freight Brokerage Business

Gift Basket Service

Growing and Selling Herbs
and Herbal Products

Home Inspection Service

Import/Export Business

Information Consultant Business

Law Practice

Lawn Care Business

Mail Order Business

Medical Claims Billing Service

Personal Training Business

Pet-Sitting Business

Restaurant and Five Other
Food Businesses

Self-Publishing Business

Seminar Production Business

Specialty Travel & Tour Business

Staffing Service

Successful Retail Business

Vending Business

Wedding Consultant Business

Wholesale Distribution Business

Entrepreneur
MAGAZINE'S

startup

2ND EDITION

Start Your Own

PERSONAL CONCIERGE SERVICE

Your Step-by-Step Guide to Success

Entrepreneur Press and Heather Heath Dismore

EP
Entrepreneur.
Press

Editorial Director: Jere L. Calmes
Managing Editor: Marla Markman
Cover Design: Beth Hansen-Winter
Production and Composition: studio Salt

This publication is designed to provide accurate and authoritative information in regard to the subject matter covered. It is sold with the understanding that the publisher is not engaged in rendering legal, accounting, or other professional services. If legal advice or other expert assistance is required, the services of a competent professional person should be sought.

Library of Congress Cataloging-in-Publication Data is available

Dismore, H. (Heather)
    Start your own personal concierge service/by Entrepreneur Press and Heather Heath Dismore.—2nd ed.
    p.   cm.
    ISBN-13: 978-1-59918-109-7 (alk. paper)
    ISBN-10: 1-59918-109-6 (alk. paper)
       1. Personal concierges. I. Addison, Lisa. Start your own personal concierge service.
II. Entrepreneur (Santa Monica, Calif.) III. Title.
HD9999.P3942.A33 2007
640—dc22   2007012864

Printed in Canada

1222618817

Contents

Preface ix

Chapter 1
Keeper of the Candles:
Industry Overview 1
Spreading Like Wildfire 2
Ancient Roots 3
Defining Moment 4
Striking While the Iron Is Hot 5
You Need That *When*? 7
Well, Isn't That Convenient? 7
Reaping the Rewards 8
Bringing Home the Bacon 8
Start Me Up 9

Chapter 2
People Who Need People:
Defining Your Market 11
Perks and More Perks 12
One Call Does It All 13

Finding Your Niche 14
What It Takes 15
   Checking Out the Competition 16
   Just for Full-Timers? 20

Chapter 3

Laying the Groundwork 23
The Name Game 24
   A Touch of Whimsy 24
   Right Where You Are 25
   Making It Official 26
Structure Is Good 26
   The Sole Proprietor 26
   A Limited Liability Company 27
   Choosing Partnerships 27
   A Corporation 27
More Than a Cubicle 29
   Home Sweet Office 29
   No Need for the Tax Man Blues 29
   Rules and Regulations 30
   Growth Spurt 30

Chapter 4

Money Is No Obstacle 35
Start-Up Costs 36
Getting Equipped 37
   Computer Choices 37
   Flashing Your Clients 38
   The Software Scene 39
   Internet Access 41
   Web Site 42
   Designing Your Web Site 42
   Hosting Your Web Site 43
   The Fine Print 43
   Just the Fax 44
   Line One Is for You 45
   Don't Miss a Call 45
   Cellular Phones and Other Gadgets 46
Getting Your Name Out 47

Start-Up Advertising 47
Getting Coverage. 49
Legal and Accounting Services 49
Is It Raining Money? 50
Getting Help 51

Chapter 5
So What Do You Do?
Daily Operations 53

Putting in the Hours 54
A Day in the Life. 54
Making Fantasies Come True 55
Filling the Bills 58
Lots of Pencil Pushing 60
Pleasing the Client 62

Chapter 6
Selling Service:
Advertising and Marketing. 63

Getting the Word Out 64
Publish a Newsletter 64
Preparing Your Elevator Speech. 65
Traditional Advertising 65
A Catch-All Phrase 66
Spinning a Web 67
Extra! Extra!. 69
Keep Them Coming Back for More. 70

Chapter 7
Who's Minding the Store?
Employees and Finances 73

Help Wanted 74
Growing Like a Weed 74
Talking Insurance 76
Benefits. 76
Watching Your Finances 77
An Important Statement 78
How Taxing 78

▲

Chapter 8

It's a Pleasure **83**

Any Regrets? 84

You're on Your Way. 85

Appendix

Personal Concierge Resources 87

Glossary **91**

Index **93**

Preface

You're the type of person who can juggle ten different projects at once and make sure they all turn out well. Everything you touch shines a little brighter when you're done. You make friends wherever you go. You thrive on deadlines and love a challenge. But after years of racing around the corporate fast track, you're ready to pursue new challenges and set your own course. And you think a personal concierge service might be your track to independence and success.

A personal concierge service runs on the most basic of premises. People want things done but don't have time to do them. But they are happy to pay someone to take care of their business efficiently and with a touch of class. Why not let that someone be you?

You are probably reading this book after thinking long and hard about starting your own business. You are excited, anxious, maybe even scared—all natural emotions when considering such a lifestyle change. Although we can't make the big leap for you, we can give you the information to help you plan your next step.

Our mission is to provide all the facts you need to:

- Decide if a personal concierge service is the right business for you.
- Promote your business for maximum results.
- Start your new business on the right foot.
- Keep your business on the track to success.

You've probably wondered what it's really like to be a personal concierge. Wouldn't it be great to actually talk to one and find out what a day in his or her life is like? What's the best part of the job? What's the most challenging? The most fun? Well, in this book you will hear from personal concierges who share their stories, tips, and a few secrets. You'll even hear some of the more unusual requests personal concierges have received. (Sorry, you'll have to wait for those tantalizing details until further along in the book.)

This business guide also includes worksheets to help you estimate start-up expenses and operating costs, ideas about organizing your business, tips on how to find and keep clients, and even a feature called Stat Fact, which highlights interesting statistics about the personal concierge industry.

We hope that you are ready to learn everything about the world of personal concierges and that you are enthusiastic about venturing into a business where you can carve out your own niche. Your new career will be exactly what you make it. And there's no reason why you can't be the next in-demand personal concierge. But first, you've got some reading to do. So jump right in. This is going to be fun!

Keeper of the Candles
Industry Overview

In this chapter, we'll explore the new trend toward personal concierge services as well as the history of the concierge profession as a whole. We'll also introduce you to several entrepreneurs who have started their own personal concierge services. You'll benefit from their experience and advice as we look into the personal concierge industry.

Spreading Like Wildfire

Concierges have been around in one form or another for centuries, but the personal concierge burst onto the scene only in the late 1990s. Today, more people have less time for everyday tasks, and many of them rely on personal concierges for everything from walking the dog to getting dinner on the table. There are few tasks a personal concierge won't tackle, as long as the chore is legal, of course.

Although personal concierge services are a fairly recent development, the number of companies that serve time-starved clients is mushrooming, right along with customer demand for such businesses. Membership in the National Association of Professional Organizers, which includes some professionals who provide concierge services, swelled from a few hundred when founded in 1985 to more than 4,000 members to date.

Why the booming demand for personal concierges and organizers? A big reason is that most people are incredibly busy with jobs, families, and/or maintaining a household. Some people need help just to get organized; others could manage the paperwork if they were not saddled with so many other chores. That is when they turn to (or would like to be able to turn to) professionals to help keep them organized, run errands, and see to it that business and personal obligations are met. They will look to personal concierges to help relieve stress and bring order to hectic lives.

Shifting Gears

Many successful concierges do not have a hotel background. In fact those interviewed for this book came from such disparate backgrounds as customer service, legal assistants, law enforcement officers, executive recruiting, and executive assistants. Kathy Strukel of Perfect Solutions in Elkhart, Indiana, travelled extensively in her former life as a paralegal. She had experience with concierges in hotels in major cities she visited and decided to bring that experience to her small town when she was looking for a life change.

Although it's no secret that the personal concierge field is booming, hard numbers are difficult to come by. The National Concierge Association, founded in Chicago in the late 1990s as a networking and resource organization for both personal and hotel concierges, doesn't yet track numbers or statistics pertaining to the industry, but membership has grown from six members in 1998 to over 600. The International Concierge and Errand Association (ICEA) boasts more than 600 members. Katharine Giovanni, a concierge and consultant, has this to say about quantifying the industry, "You can actually see the phenomenal growth by looking at my company's numbers. Triangle Concierge began in 1998 with a dozen clients. Today we have thousands of clients from 40 countries and every U.S. state." Several other personal concierges and concierge consultants agreed with that estimate and said the number of personal concierges is growing fast.

Fun Fact

The National Concierge Association (NCA) defines the title of *concierge* as an individual whose principal occupational responsibility is to facilitate, or to arrange for the facilitation of, any request placed by a client, visitor, guest, or tenant, providing the request is legal, ethical, and appropriate for the concierge to do.

According to Sara-Ann Kasner, president and founder of the National Concierge Association, "The concierge business is exploding right now. There has been tremendous growth." Personal concierges and industry analysts say there is plenty of room for even more growth.

Ancient Roots

Although more and more people are becoming familiar with the term "concierge," very few know where this customer service-based profession originated. The word "concierge" evolved from the French comte des cierges, the "keeper of the candles," a term that referred to the servant who attended to the whims of visiting noblemen at medieval castles. Eventually, the name "concierge" came to stand for the keepers of the keys at public buildings, especially hotels. There is even a famous prison in Paris that is called The Conciergerie, in honor of the warden who kept the keys and assigned cells to the inmates.

Service personnel known as concierges first showed up in some luxury hotels in Europe in the early 1900s. Then, as now, their duties were to welcome and assist guests throughout their stay. Naturally, guests didn't have as many options or services as they do today. Traditionally, male concierges were mostly found in the better hotels. Today, there are as many female as male concierges in the United States, while in Europe the concierge industry remains predominantly male.

▲

Fun Fact

The U.S. branch of the Les Clefs d'Or have hosted, sponsored, and led symposia and full semester-long courses at many of the most prestigious hospitality programs in the country, including Cornell University, University of Nevada-Las Vegas, Penn State, and Johnson & Wales.

Defining Moment

To fully understand the industry, it's important to make the distinction between hotel concierges, corporate concierges, and personal concierges (we'll be focusing on the latter in this book).

Hotel concierges are employed by hotels to assist guests by arranging tours, making dinner reservations, offering advice on shopping or sightseeing, and taking care of other needs that may arise during their stay. At this time, only hotel concierges may become members of the elite Les Clefs d'Or (pronounced "lay clay door"), a professional organization of hotel concierges all over the world. To join, applicants must have at least five years of hotel experience with at least two of those years as a lobby concierge. Applicants must also pass a written test, submit letters of recommendation, and pass test calls by examiners who pose as hotel guests.

Of the approximately 5,000 hotel concierges in the United States, 160 applied to join Les Clefs d'Or in a recent year, and only 25 were accepted. Les Clefs d'Or means "the keys of gold," and it's the emblem adopted by the association of concierges founded in Paris in 1929. Hence the gold keys pins that you will see on the lapels of concierges who are members of Les Clefs d'Or. If a hotel concierge is ever found guilty of an ethical breach, such as accepting commissions from restaurants or other companies, he or she is banned from the group for life and must surrender the gold keys.

Corporate concierges are employed by a corporation to serve the firm's employees. The niche for corporate concierges grew out of the desire of some corporations to keep their employees so happy that they would never leave for greener pastures. In the quest for worker satisfaction, some companies have hired concierges to help employees, with planning business trips, picking up dry cleaning, ordering dinner, running errands, and so on. Dentists, psychologists, massage therapists, and others are even offering their services in the workplace through concierges.

A personal concierge is not employed by a hotel or a corporation. Instead, these men and women market their services directly to clients who pay them for running errands, buying gifts, making travel arrangements, or myriad other tasks. Some of their clients may, however, be corporations which contract with them to be available for employee requests.

While personal concierges typically appeal to a different market than those in hotels or corporations, their markets sometimes overlap. For instance, a businessperson may use the services of a hotel concierge while traveling and the services of a personal concierge after returning home.

Typically, a personal concierge builds a client base that uses his or her services on a regular basis. Clients might mostly be individual consumers, or predominately small businesses. They could even be a combination of the two. The personal concierge business is so new and evolving so quickly that no hard and fast rules exist. Again, this business is definitely what you make it. (You'll read more about defining the personal concierge market in Chapter 2.)

Striking While the Iron Is Hot

Whether it's because of time constraints or just a need for convenience, more and more consumers are turning to personal concierges in an effort to streamline their lives. Again, no official numbers are available on just how many people work as personal concierges, but consider these facts:

- More and more hotel concierges, after learning every aspect of the trade, are walking away from their jobs to start their own personal concierge businesses.
- The internet has made it easier for entrepreneurs to succeed in far-flung fields. For example, the internet allows a personal concierge in Idaho to target potential clients in Louisiana—or even Paris.
- Several concierge networks and associations exist today, when just one was around 10 years ago.

Personal concierges who live in small towns or who reach out to clients outside their immediate geographic area generally have contacts and resources near those locations to handle the hands on work. Ida Stanley, founder of Concierges Connections, has developed what she calls, "an affiliated network that is all encompassing, bridging the gap between clients and premier concierge providers." Her network matches up clients with a concierge located in the area where they need service.

Concierge businesses can offer a smorgasbord of services or specialize in one or two areas. For instance, some personal concierges organize clients' cluttered desks, set up their offices, and help them manage their schedules. Others offer to do everything from standing in line at the Department of Motor

Stat Fact
Where does the time go? A recent survey, by the nonprofit research organization Families and Work Institute said 52 percent of workers feel they don't have enough time to get their work done, compared to 40 percent in 1977. The same study indicates 78 percent of couples live in a two-income family, working a combined total 91 hours per week. Personal concierges can count on getting more business as people look to relieve the stress and maximize their time away from the office.

Stat Fact

According to a recent survey by the U.S. Bureau of Labor Statistics, there are more than 33 million two-income families (Statistics). If everyone in a household is working, nobody has time to run errands—so business is likely to pick up for personal concierges.

Vehicles to helping set up an elaborate marriage proposal. Some concierge businesses specialize in wedding planning, shopping for and wrapping gifts, and decorating for the holidays. Some offer pet-sitting services. Other specialize in elder care services, like accompanying seniors to doctors appointments, picking up prescriptions, or driving them to hair appointments. The list of services is endless, and it changes every day.

One reason more people are using the services of personal concierges is that their free time is fading away faster than ever. As a rule, most of us have less personal time than in years past. How many times have you heard the refrain "There just aren't enough hours in the day"? Hence, the demand for helpers to run errands for us. More than ever, families include two full-time wage earners, and even many teenagers hold down part-time jobs. Who will get dinner on the table, pick up the dry cleaning, get the dog groomed, and make sure the lawn gets mowed on a regular basis if everyone is at work? Can you say "concierge?"

According to the concierges interviewed for this book, people who make the best concierges share certain characteristics: They're patient, calm, resourceful, have good contacts, and enjoy people. If that sounds like you, and you like having a different routine every day, juggling multiple projects, and making people happy, this could be the business for you. We'll talk a lot more about what it takes to be a concierge and explore a typical day in the life of a concierge in Chapter 5.

Concierge Conundrum

A client orders a special piece of jewelry and asks his personal concierge to pick up the piece so he can present it to his wife at a dinner party that evening. The concierge gets to the store and finds it closed for inventory. Panic? Not a concierge. He pulls out his Rolodex and gets busy. It takes two hours, but he eventually locates the owner of the store who agrees to open it so the concierge can retrieve the jewelry. The client? None the wiser. He gets his piece of jewelry on time. The wife? Happy as a clam. The concierge? Ends up with a fat tip.

Some personal concierges say the field was so new when they started their businesses that there were few experts to turn to for advice. The few people already established in the field were often reluctant to give away any secrets for fear of competition. As the field grew, more resources became available to anyone looking for ideas about setting up a personal concierge business; you can find some of these listed in the Appendix of this book.

You Need That *When?*

A personal concierge's duties can be as simple as gift-shopping for a client or as elaborate as arranging to have a Rolls Royce waiting at the airport to whisk a client and his girlfriend to a hotel room stocked with six dozen red roses, chilled champagne, a catered prime rib dinner, and a camera to record her reaction when he proposes.

Personal concierges are people with connections. They know how to get front-row tickets to a concert that has been sold out for weeks. They know whom to call when a client isn't happy with the color of his rental car and wants a fire-engine red convertible delivered now. They don't panic when a client calls with a last-minute request for a private jet. They have Rolodexes that read like a who's who. And most important, they perform well under pressure and almost always get the job done—politely and with a smile.

Personal concierges aren't just for people with deep pockets. Time-saving perks are enjoyed by all sorts. In a sense, people who employ a personal concierge are buying back their own time, and who can't benefit from that? A personal concierge's clients might include everyone from corporate millionaires and hot-shot celebrities to couples with two incomes but zero free time to single moms holding down two jobs. One client may require the services of a personal concierge only a couple of hours a month, while another client may insist that the concierge be available at all times.

Well, Isn't That Convenient?

According to the concierges interviewed for this book, most people don't have a clear picture of what a concierge is. Many people understand the concept once you explain it to them, and think it's a great business idea. Jennifer C. of Gainesville, Georgia, says she was "shocked that [potential clients] didn't pick up on it as expected. I spend a lot of time educating them about what we do, teaching people about my business. You have to break them of the habit of doing the errands themselves. Once they get used to you, they can't live without you."

Kathy S. in Elkhart, Indiana, knows it's important to anticipate clients' needs before they even voice them. She tells of one client who works from home, but travels extensively. "I take care of her cat quite a bit. Once she was out of town and I noticed she was running low on her favorite tea. I made sure she was restocked before she returned home."

Stat Fact

44 percent of workers are over-worked some of the time or most of the time, according to a recent study by the Families and Work Institute. What does this mean for personal concierges? The less free time clients have, the more likely they are to rely on concierge services.

Reaping the Rewards

Almost every concierge we talked to loved their job and are so glad they took the plunge. One concierge worked with lawyers in her previous profession and found that they were always critical. In her current business, every-thing she does makes her clients happy. "I love knowing that what I'm doing means something to people." Another notes the vari-ety as key to her job satisfaction, "I face a new challenge every day, and it keeps my brain fresh. Also, there is a great privilege associ-ated with earning a client's trust enough that they allow you access to their most personal affairs."

Even though being a personal concierge is, by all accounts, a rewarding job, it can also be a stressful one. "The hardest thing about the job is keeping all the details straight," says Cynthia A., the concierge in San Diego. "You have a lot of balls in the air; the more successful you are, the more balls you have in the air."

Think of a concierge as someone who can attend to the little—and the big—details of life for people who don't have the time to attend to the details themselves.

Bringing Home the Bacon

Personal concierges can expect to make anywhere from $10,000 to $60,000 a year, conservatively. (Once they've built a clientele, $40,000 to $60,000 each year is more realistic for those working full time). However, businesses with annual incomes of $125,000 or more are not unheard of, depending on their location, the clients they take on, and the range of services they offer. In addition, concierges often receive tips or gifts from grateful clients.

Concierges bill their clients in a variety of ways. For instance, some charge mem-bership fees based on how many requests are usually made per month. Others bill on monthly retainers, while others charge per service or per hour. Most we spoke to billed by the hour. It's your game, and you can tailor it to meet your needs.

When asked to put numbers to their fees, concierges say their typical charges work out to be anywhere from $15 to $125 an hour, depending on the particular task and the geographic location of your business. For example, rates are typically higher in urban areas than in rural areas. If concierges dip into their own money to purchase something for a client, the client is billed for the item later.

Some personal concierges also receive what are known as referral fees from vari-ous companies when they steer business to them. Companies that often pay referral fees include wedding planners, caterers, and florists. Many concierges will pick up extra income via this avenue.

Start Me Up

By now, you must be wondering what kind of hard cash it takes to get started in the personal concierge business. As with many busi-

Fun Fact
Did you know that concierges often rub elbows with celebrities? Shhh, don't tell anyone. Concierges never do.

nesses, it all depends on how you decide to get started.

Start-up costs for a personal concierge business are estimated to be between $500 and $5,000, (if you already have a computer and other office basics, such as a printer and fax machine). If not, the figure could be considerably higher, depending on what kind of computer system and other office supplies you choose to buy.

Since it is a service-based business rather than a product-based one that calls for inventory, starting a personal concierge business doesn't require a large financial investment. In fact, much of what you'll need to be a good concierge can't be bought—for instance, the contacts that come from long-term business relationships with the right people. You can't put a price tag on those contacts, but having them puts you well on the way to success.

You'll still need all the basics, though. In addition to a computer, items such as office supplies, reference materials, postage, stationery, business cards, phone, voice mail, and internet access are vital. We'll have a lot more on equipping your office in Chapter 4.

Ready for the next step? In Chapter 2, we take a look at just how hot the personal concierge market is and why personal concierges are popping up just about everywhere, including the corporate world.

People Who Need People
Defining Your Market

Who uses personal concierges? Everyone from the millionaire corporate chairperson to the single mom with two jobs and three children under age ten. In a sense, people who employ a personal concierge are buying back their own time, and who can't benefit from that? This chapter shows you how important it is to identify your prospective clients and determine what services you will provide for them.

Although the term "concierge" used to be associated mostly with upscale hotels, concierges are now found in many different settings. In this chapter, we'll show you some of the settings where you'll find concierges, and we'll look at some of the hottest trends in the industry. Keep your brain churning so you can dream up just the niche for you. The options are endless!

Perks and More Perks

In today's competitive job market, employers are finding that they not only need to create a safe and supportive environment for their employees, but that they must also give employees benefits that help them balance the demands of work and personal commitments. Some companies have found that their employees are putting in so much overtime, committing to crazy business travel schedules, and working such long hours that they don't have enough hours left in the week to attend to personal business. Employers in certain fields, such as insurance, banking, and manufacturing, have found that offering help to their time-stretched employees can boost productivity, making this a workplace perk that benefits the business as well as the workers.

For this reason, more employers are offering personal concierge services to their employees. If an employee knows he won't have time to cook or stop for dinner on the way home from work, he can pick up the phone and call his company's personal concierge service to order dinner and have it delivered—leaving the work to the concierge. Or if the salesperson is on the road and has to extend her trip another few days, she can pick up the phone and make sure her landscaping needs are taken care of while she's gone. Industry experts predict we'll be seeing more and more personal concierges serving businesses in the near future. These personal concierges are not to be confused with corporate concierges; they are not actually corporate employees—more like corporate suppliers. Personal concierge operators are contracted by corporations to provide concierge services, either on-site or on call.

Stat Fact

According to *Entrepreneur* magazine and Pricewaterhouse-Coopers' first annual "Entrepreneurial Challenges Survey," 73 percent of the founders and CEOs of 340 fast-growth businesses surveyed said retaining key workers was the biggest issue they faced. Adding a personal concierge to the list of perks might just help employees keep their work/life balance in check, and ultimately keep them at their job.

Every concierge we spoke with believes that the outlook for the concierge market is bright. Loreine G., The Errand Genie, notes, "The industry is going to necessarily boom as more and more households turn into dual income homes and individuals find themselves needing qualified, capable, and efficient help to complete tasks." Abbie M. goes back to educating people about the service, "It's certainly something people are looking for, they just don't know what it is, what to look for. In the next 10 years, the industry can only grow as people become more aware. We are constantly hearing about how busy we all are and how long we work. A huge majority of the population will start using a personal concierge, just as they have house cleaners and gardeners."

Stat Fact

A study published in the American Management Association's *Compensation & Benefits Review* found most corporations that responded to its survey had some sort of work site convenience. Nearly 30 percent offered on-site gift stores, for example, and 22 percent had on-site medical care. Others used the services of personal concierges for their employees.

Kellye G. sees concierges in the "lobbies of office buildings, offered in employee compensation packages, and in hospitals." It's just one more tool corporations are finding helpful in a competitive job market as they try to woo potential candidates to their companies—and then try to keep employees happy once they're on board.

Even if you don't have a contract with a corporation, you can still target many corporate employees who need some extra help. For instance, one savvy personal concierge set up shop in a corner of a busy Chicago office building and specialized in filling grocery orders for busy secretaries and executives who never had time to get their food shopping done. She had helpers who bought the nonperishables and returned with them by the end of the day. The enterprising concierge then had other helpers load everything up into her van, which she set up in the employee parking lot as her clients were leaving work. Her clients picked up their groceries; she picked up her checks—and everyone was happy.

One Call Does It All

Another hot new trend is the emergence of personal concierges in the real estate world. Some real estate brokerage firms are contracting personal concierge services to connect home buyers with internet, cable, gas, electric, and security system installations, plus newspaper and recycling services—and the homebuyer makes only a single phone call. What's not to like about that? (Hint: This could be a good place for new personal concierges to get a start.)

▲

Many real estate firms put together a network of local vendors, such as dry cleaners, florists, and bakers, who offer the real estate customers services at discounted prices. Many are expanding these services to include full relocation services like restaurant recommendations, interior design consulting, salon recommendations, locating childcare providers, and assistance with locating places of worship. A personal concierge can become the link between the real estate customer and the dozens (or hundreds) of vendors on the brokerage's list, allowing the customer to take care of dozens of errands with just one phone call.

Real estate giant Coldwell Banker has developed its own service, Coldwell Banker Concierge, to help its clients move seamlessly from one home to another. Services range from locksmithing, carpet installations, and maid service to providing feng shui masters. Personal concierges increasingly provide the bridge between customers and the services being offered by real estate firms. You could be the provider for a smaller boutique real estate broker in your area that wants to provide premier service to his clients.

Some experts predict it won't be long before the concierge concept will be in virtually every real estate market in the country. In fact, some real estate companies have already begun referring to themselves as being in the home services business instead of the real estate business.

And the trend doesn't stop with residential real estate. As revitalization of downtown areas occurs across the country, more people are choosing downtown living, often in high rise condos and luxury apartments. You could provide services for tenants in those buildings. If you can make inroads with a developer in your area, you could specialize in servicing these locations. You do realize what this means for you, right? Just one more niche you can specialize in! And with the field exploding the way it is, you can expect that similar opportunities may crop up down the road.

If you want to start a personal concierge business in the real estate industry, you could offer to provide some of the services we mentioned above. For instance, if you have sources who know a lot about feng shui, you might offer feng shui; if you have some contacts in the locksmith field, think about providing locksmithing services. Again, the possibilities are absolutely endless.

Finding Your Niche

As an aspiring personal concierge, you need to decide what your niche will be. For instance, will you cater strictly to corporate clients? Will you specialize in particular areas for clients or offer more broad-based services? Some personal concierges specialize in one area, such as lining up tickets for concerts or special events; others pride themselves on running every errand imaginable. You need to spend some time thinking about what type of service you want to provide.

After thinking about what you want to do, take it a step further and write out a formal mission statement for your business. The statement should define your goals and lay out your plans for your business. See the Mission Statement Worksheet on page 17 for help getting started on your own.

Kellye G., the personal concierge in Ft. Worth, Texas, notes that finding her niche was one of the biggest challenges when she started her business. "It took a solid month and the luck of a perfect referral," she says, to get her on the path to success. On a typical day, she spends 9AM–1PM with a permanent weekday client, then spends the afternoon working with other clients and building her business through prospecting for clients, writing proposals, and updating her web site.

Loreine G., The Errand Genie, has found her niche by handling two categories of tasks, "errand running (shopping, dry cleaning, etc.) and time consuming tasks such as expense report preparation, vendor research, form preparation, and submission," for both corporate clients and individuals. She notes, "My typical client, regardless of industry, is young, professional, type A personality with pressing time demands."

Katharine G. says that her clients are almost exclusively corporate clients and that her company often provides errand services. "We'll pick up people's groceries and prescriptions, go to the post office, do light—and I emphasize light—housekeeping, make phone calls, personal shopping, pick up meals, and run various other errands," Katharine says. "We also do event planning, weddings, parties, expos, and things of that nature. And we have a business referral service that is very popular."

"I think personal concierges help to take the stress off of people's shoulders," says Katharine. "The need for concierges has arisen from the simple fact that we are all just so busy today."

Kathy Stukel of Elkhart, Indiana, has found a niche for herself by catering to the families of students at nearby Notre Dame University. They deliver chicken soup baskets to sick students, plan tailgate parties, arrange exam time snack baskets, and coordinate travel arrangements.

What It Takes

A good dose of business savvy goes a long way in this business. Most concierges we spoke with had challenges with starting a new business, just like anyone would regardless of industry. "The first year of any business is very difficult. You must work really hard and spend

Tip...

Smart Tip

There is no point in trying to make all your clients fit into one neat little category, especially if you don't intend to specialize in the corporate arena. Your clients may be family members, old friends, the pediatrician who has known you since you were 3, your sixth-grade teacher's next-door neighbor. You get the idea—the possibilities are endless. Keep an open mind, keep an eye out for new possibilities, and then watch your business soar.

▲

a lot of money on advertising that doesn't always pay off initially. You are constantly having to prove yourself to establish the trust that this industry demands," notes one concierge fairly new to the industry. Ida Stanley of Concierges Connection says her biggest challenge was actually running the business. She overcame them by, "building an entire operating system that now has an operating manual, which includes marketing and sales procedures and materials as well as all segments of a concierge business owner's daily operation." She sells the system to aspiring concierges (see the Appendix for contact information).

Checking Out the Competition

Even if you are the only concierge in town, you will probably always have competition. Who is your competition? Well, it might be professional organizers, errand-running companies, and those who offer specialized services, such as dog-sitters, house-sitters, etc.

And although you might be the only concierge in town, don't forget that large concierge services have the resources to reach out and advertise all over the United States. So even though the business owner might live six states away, a larger personal concierge service could still tap into business in your city. Let's face it, a company with 40 employees will be able to provide services a one-person company cannot. But if you

---

On a Mission

When you're starting a business, it's very important to have a mission statement—that's a fancy term for defining your company's goals and laying out exactly how you plan to achieve those goals. There isn't a blueprint for the perfect mission statement. It's up to you to decide what you want to include. But you could use the following example to get you started.

ACE Concierge will always put the client first. Our aim is to provide services to everyone from upscale corporate clients to busy stay-at-home moms. By virtue of our professionalism, enthusiasm, and customer service, we will become known as the foremost concierge service in Mayberry, Ohio. Our goal is to have 15 clients within our first year of business.

As you can see, your mission statement doesn't have to be long and wordy—but it's crucial that you have one. It shows you have spent some time figuring out what type of company you want to have and what kinds of services you will offer. And it proves you're serious about your business and about establishing a good reputation.

Mission Statement Worksheet

Use this worksheet to create your own mission statement. It should include the following basic elements:

- ○ A look at the part of the concierge market your business will serve and a description of how you want the community to view your company
- ○ A look at how you want your clients to perceive your company
- ○ A look into the future—where you want your business to be in one year, five years, ten years

Mission Statement for _____

(your company's name)

_____
_____
_____
_____
_____
_____
_____
_____
_____
_____
_____
_____
_____
_____
_____
_____
_____
_____
_____
_____
_____
_____
_____

are that one-person company, there are ways you can compete, such as giving your undivided attention to clients and being there at the drop of a hat when needed. Remember: Customer service is the name of the game.

You don't have to be all things to all people, though. As long as your clients are happy, that's what counts. Focus on providing more "personal" service to your clients; after all, that is what many of them are paying you for.

Competition is an issue you'll certainly have to address when you start your business. Some concierges we talked to believe there is enough business to go around, while others are nervous that, with the industry growing so quickly, competitors might soon be infringing on their territory. Two concierges recently crossed paths in a small Connecticut area and agreed to split up their territory, giving referrals to the other when appropriate. They aren't formal partners, but each helps build the other's business rather than infringe on it. And you don't need to be geographically close to help each other out. Jennifer Cochran and Jackie Murphy live in different states, but often help each other review forms and advertising pieces, among other things. The internet offers a great way to "get to know" others in this growing industry even if you're not operating in the same geographic area. Jennifer is the moderator of the Yahoo! Groups Errand Services, an online forum designed to help errand runners share ideas and information. "It's not about competition. The more we work together, the more the industry is going to grow. Overall that's better for everyone. We get recognition when our industry is in the news. You can clip that *Wall Street Journal* article about the industry and put it into your sales package you deliver to your local hospital" to help them see the scope of the industry and possibly contract you to provide the same service to their patients.

So what types of market research do personal concierges need to do? Most of the ones we talked to did engage in some market research. As you'll read throughout this book, each entrepreneur had to carve out his or her own niche and wing it. There really is no blueprint for this business. Those who have been around 10 or more yearsreally made their own path. Many are willing to share their secrets with you, for a fee of course, so check out the Appendix for information on getting in touch with them and pursuing your education in this exciting new field.

Some of these concierges spent time checking out their local markets and looking in the Yellow Pages to see what types of similar services were out there. Often, they found no other businesses offering what they planned to offer, which meant the field was wide open and primed for their success. But they still needed to find out whether people were interested in what they had to offer. Some concierges sent out sales letters they designed themselves. They sent the letters to potential clients culled from business listings in the phone book or referrals from friends or family.

Today, there is a little more help for people who want to start personal concierge services. Katharine Giovanni of Triangle Concierge in Raleigh, North Carolina, says she receives dozens of calls each month from people interested in starting their own services. In addition to providing concierge services, Katharine's company trains would-be concierges at its Triangle Concierge Masters Academy at 1- and 3-day group seminars, or one-on-one training sessions. Kathy S. from Elkhart took the 3-day training from Triangle Concierge. She noted, "Katharine Giovanni is the guru of this industry. I was mesmerized during training."

For those who can't travel to seminar locations, you can purchase materials (like training tools, software, must-have forms, and client management tools) or consult directly with it via telephone by appointment at competitive rates. The company also gives tips on various aspects of the personal concierge business, including skills for being successful, setting your fees, dealing with service vendors and commissions, and understanding legal and accounting issues. We've also provided a worksheet on page 20 to give you ideas on how to start your research. You can never have too much info when it comes to marketing your business.

Just for Full-Timers?

Now, what about someone who may want to work as a personal concierge—but only on a part-time basis? Again, overwhelmingly, the concierges we talked to were full time and completely immersed in the business. But most agreed that since the business—as well as your clients—can be tailored to your specific needs and desires, you can certainly make a go of it as a part-timer. The only problem most of the concierges could foresee was that some of your clients might want you to be available full time.

But with today's technology, there is no reason you can't be available to your clients. You can give them a phone number, fax number, and e-mail address where they can reach you any time; of course, this will only work if you do your part and check your messages, faxes, and e-mails often. One of the most exciting things about the personal concierge business is that it really is what you make it.

Market Research Checklist

Need a few ideas to get you started on your market research? This list can help you get organized and coordinate your efforts.

Target Your Market

❑ Identify five markets you'd like to target.

1. _____

2. _____

3. _____

4. _____

5. _____

❑ Make calls to the businesses or individuals you've identified.

❑ Send out surveys to get ideas about what services would be appreciated.

❑ Follow up phone calls and returned surveys with thank-you notes.

❑ Schedule interviews with interested potential clients.

❑ Bring a copy of your survey to use in your interviews.

❑ Follow up interviews with thank-you notes or calls.

Research the Demographics

❑ Find out everything you can about the neighborhood, town, or county in which you wish to operate.

❑ Get on the internet.

❑ Talk to neighbors.

❑ Read local papers.

❑ Check with your local librarian.

Find Your Niche

❑ Choose three unique areas that will make your business stand out.

1. _____

2. _____

3. _____

How Can I Help You?

Here's a list of some of the services personal concierges can offer. Of course, with the industry growing and developing the way it is, it's impossible to give a complete list. Who knows what new service might be offered next week? But this list might help you come up with a few ideas for services you can provide to your clients.

Personal/Family Services

- ○ Forgotten lunches/homework/gym clothes pick up/drop off
- ○ Interior decorating
- ○ Landscaping
- ○ Providing maid service
- ○ Carpet cleaning
- ○ Video store pick up/drop off
- ○ Library runs
- ○ Invitation & card writing
- ○ Pet sitting
- ○ Light housekeeping
- ○ Waiting in line at the DMV
- ○ Taking cars in for repair, oil changes, car washes
- ○ Event planning
- ○ Gift buying
- ○ Taking care of plants
- ○ Picking up dry cleaning
- ○ Doing grocery shopping
- ○ Locating hard-to-find items and collectibles
- ○ Picking up mail
- ○ Picking up meals; providing chef services
- ○ Making reservations

Luxury/VIP Services

- ○ Hotel and restaurant reservations
- ○ Meeting and event planning
- ○ Corporate and personal travel
- ○ Yacht and fishing charters
- ○ Gift baskets and floral deliveries
- ○ Executive retreats
- ○ Meet and greet at the airport for clients
- ○ Organizing itineraries for clients
- ○ Theater and entertainment tickets
- ○ Golf tournaments and tee times
- ○ Transportation
- ○ Reminder service
- ○ VIP experiences

Corporate

- ○ Personal research and special projects
- ○ Mobile notary
- ○ Making travel arrangements
- ○ Virtual assistant service
- ○ Mystery shopper for retail and restaurants
- ○ Complete expense reports

Relocation Services

- ○ Packing/unpacking
- ○ Move-in-day assistance
- ○ Home staging/decluttering/ organizing
- ○ Connecting utilities
- ○ Referring landscaping, contractors, painters, etc.
- ○ Change of address notification

Laying the
Groundwork

This chapter will help you understand how to structure your business and give you tips on everything from naming your business to finding a location for your office. Don't worry if you're the type who would rather have a root canal than deal with legal forms and zoning regulations, because we've done our best to make this relatively pain free for you.

The Name Game

Deciding what to name your business is one of the most important things you should have on your to-do list. The name you finally settle on will be what potential clients see when thumbing through the phone book, looking at your business card, or checking out an advertisement about your service.

Yes, the name should be catchy and memorable, but it should also clearly convey exactly what your business is. A very clever name that tells absolutely nothing about your business would defeat the purpose. Your goal in choosing a business name should go way beyond showing the world how creative you are.

Because customer service is a benchmark of the personal concierge business, the name of your business could play up that angle. How about something like "At Your Service" or "We Put You First"? You could also go the sophisticated route and use terminology common to the concierge or service industry. For instance, words like "elite," "courtesy," or "professional" could be used in the name of your business. Brainstorm and come up with some good words or key phrases. Kathy Stukel of Elkhart, Indiana, chose The Perfect Solutions after brainstorming extensively about the service she wanted to supply to her clients and then looking at available domain names for her web site.

When Abbie Martin, owner of Lifestyle Elements in Torrance, Australia, was developing her name, she relied on her previous work experience, "With my marketing background, I knew it was important to have a name which would carry my business through all its different incarnations. So I tried to think about how I would like to see my business in 5, 10, 20 years and worked from there. I wanted to provide a business which serviced all the different elements in my clients' lives."

When one personal concierge was starting her business, many of her friends and family encouraged her to leave the word "concierge" out of the name, telling her she should stick with something more familiar to most people. But she rejected that advice and named her business Concierge At Large. "I knew how important it was to have the name concierge in the title," she says. "I would never have considered not having the name in the title."

A Touch of Whimsy

A current trend is to choose a more whimsical name. Examples include the Errand Hopper in Denver, Errand Van Goes in Virginia Beach, It's About Time Concierge and Errand service in Cincinnati, Ms. Errands in Springfield, and Better than a Butler in Memphis.

Others incorporate their own name in a clever way, like See Katie Run in Walnut Creek, California, owned and operated by Katie Owensby. Jennifer Ferri runs, The Ferri Godmother, in Middlefield, Connecticut. Jillian Holmquist's personal concierge business is titled QuistAssist, playing off her last name.

Some choose whimsical names because they have a special meaning to them. Loreine G. chose her name, the Errand Genie, because, "We wanted something that honored my Middle Eastern heritage, but still conveyed the idea of errand running and speed." Jennifer Cochran of Warp Speed Errands chose her name because, "I'm a huge Star Trek fan. Warp speed is the speed that ships travel in space [on the TV show], so it just fit. It came to me in an epiphany. I run errands fast, so 'Warp Speed' works."

Right Where You Are

Some business owners like to incorporate the name of their town or a distinctive feature of the area when naming their business. Kellye Garrett of Cowtown Concierge Services named her business after the nickname for her hometown of Ft. Worth, Texas. Ida Stanley chose her name, North Coast Concierge, because the Cleveland area is recognized locally as the North Coast. Concierge by the Sea operates in the coastal community of Lewes, Delaware. Indy Errands Girls operates out of (you guessed it) Indianapolis.

> ### ⚠ Beware!
> In addition to checking the Yellow Pages, it's always a good idea to check out local business guides and directories of area networking clubs before settling on a name for your business. You can't use a name someone else is already using, and you don't want a name that could be easily confused with another business. And don't forget to check the internet to see if the matching web site address (also known as a *domain name*) is available. It's as easy as typing in your potential business name into your favorite search engine, like this—www.yourpotentialbusinessname.com—and watch what happens.

Using concierge in the title paired with a geographic indicator makes a simple name and could work well in this industry. One personal concierge said it was "a complete no-brainer" when it came to naming her business. "We live in an area that has three main cities and the area is known as the Triangle," she says. "So when it came time to name our business we just had to go with the name Triangle Concierge. Nothing else would have made sense. It says where we're from and what we do."

Put your thinking cap on, use your imagination, and remember that some of your best options for a business name are familiar features, places, or ideas. Enlist family and friends to help you come up with the perfect name. Have a small group over for a casual dinner and toss around some names to see what kinds of reactions you get. If your creativity needs a jump-start, take a look at the personal concierge services in the Appendix. Sorry, you can't borrow any of those names for your business, but the bright ideas should provide some wonderful inspiration for you. You can also use the worksheet we've provided on page 28 to help get you going.

Of course, you should definitely consider whether the name or the initials of the business have a double meaning. For instance, make sure the initials don't spell out

Bright Idea

Some enterprising business owners purposely choose a name for their business that begins with the letter "A" so it will come first in phone books and other lists.

something inappropriate or something that could be misconstrued. On the other hand, perhaps the initials spell out a slogan for your new business. For example, Associated Concierge Experts would have the initials ACE. Therefore, you could bill yourself as an "ace concierge."

Making It Official

Since you want the name of your business to be unique, it's always a good idea to check your local business directories and Yellow Pages before settling on a name. Make sure no one else is using the same name or one similar enough to cause confusion to potential clients.

Once you have a name picked out, the next step is to register it as your dba (doing business as), or "fictitious business name." This is usually a fairly simple procedure that ensures someone else isn't already using the name you've chosen. If nobody else is using it, you may pay a fee to register the name as yours. If someone else already has dibs on the name, you can move to the next name on your list.

The procedure to register a name can vary depending on where you live. In some states, it's as simple as visiting the county clerk's office, while in other states you may need to check in with the office of the secretary of state.

In any case, it's generally not a time-consuming procedure and usually involves nothing more than filling out a registration form, paying a registration fee, and turning in a form from your local newspaper that shows you have advertised your fictitious business name. Registration fees are usually inexpensive, although fees can vary by state and region.

Structure Is Good

Now that your business has a name, it needs a structure. You have the option of operating your new business as a sole proprietorship, an LLC (a Limited Liability Company), a partnership, or corporation.

The Sole Proprietor

A sole proprietorship is an option if you have no partners. The set up is extremely simple, in fact in most towns you don't need to fill out specific paperwork to declare your business a sole proprietorship. (You of course need to fill out other paperwork to get things like a business license and a dba certificate, but not to specifically form a sole proprietorship). But the downside is that your personal assets aren't protected if your business is sued. So, if you have an employee running errands and that employee hits a pedestrian, you as the business owner may lose business *and* personal assets if a judgment is placed against your sole proprietorship. That means depending on the size of the judgment and the kind of liability insurance you have, you could lose your home, your kid's college funds, and the like.

Bright Idea

Start a file for your business associates' contact information. Organize it by business type or profession for easy use. That way, when you need to call your attorney, accountant, or a new client, the number is at your fingertips.

A Limited Liability Company

An LLC is similar to a sole proprietorship, but it offers a legal way to keep your personal assets separate from your business obligations. It offers protection of your home, your bank accounts, and other assets in the event that your business experiences an unforeseen tragedy. As the name suggests, it limits your liability in a tough financial situation.

Choosing Partnerships

Most personal concierges that were interviewed for this book set up their businesses as sole proprietorships or LLCs, but you may want to go a different route. It's important to look at all of your options so you can determine the best choice for your own situation.

Cynthia A., the personal concierge from San Diego, structured her business as a partnership and says it works like a charm because she found the right partners. "I have two partners, and we just function so well together that everything runs almost perfectly," she says. "One of us is good at one area of the business, while the others are good in other areas. It's a great balance. As far as the legal aspects of a partnership, I'd definitely advise anyone to go through an attorney because there are complicated aspects to it and there is a lot of paperwork. As for the emotional aspects or the rewards, I think that when you have a partnership, everyone puts equal effort into the business and each person cares about it as much as the others. That's how it should work, anyway."

A Corporation

Most personal concierges qualify to become S Corporations, which means they can structure their business as a corporation, but avoid some of the tax consequences of a standard C corporation. With a standard corporation, the corporation pays tax, then the shareholders (in this case you) pay tax on what the corporation pays you (your salary), in effect you pay taxes twice as a standard C Corporation. To be an S Corporation, you need less than 100 shareholders and meet a few different criteria.

Business Name Worksheet

List five business name ideas associated with the type of service you plan to provide as a personal concierge. For instance: professional, efficient, detailed.

1. _____ 2. _____

3. _____ 4. _____

5. _____

List five business name ideas based on the region of the country where you live. You can use the name of your town or state, for example. Think about something your area is known for. Remember Cowtown Concierge and North Coast Concierge we talked about? Have fun with it.

1. _____ 2. _____

3. _____ 4. _____

5. _____

List five business names that are clever or whimsical. Remember to consider your name, your types of services, and the image you're trying to communicate to prospective clients. Use your imagination.

1. _____ 2. _____

3. _____ 4. _____

5. _____

OK, you've spent some time narrowing down your choices. You think you've decided which name is right for you. Now you need to:

○ Write it out one more time for good measure and then take a look at the initials; make sure they don't spell out something inappropriate. Say it out loud to hear what it sounds like. Run the name by family and friends to see if they're as impressed with it as you are.

○ Check out the web site address to make sure it's available.

○ Check with your county clerk's office to make sure the name isn't already in use.

○ Consult your local Yellow Pages to ensure another business doesn't have the same or similar name.

○ Let everyone know that you've officially named your new business!

More Than a Cubicle

It's a fact that you will need an office, whether it's located in your home or else-where. There are plenty of choices available for your office setup—executive suites, home offices, and alternative offices (such as sharing office space with another profes-sional). We'll take a look at some of those choices in this section.

No matter where your office is located, it's important that your clients get a good impression when dealing with you. That first impression is very important because it might make or break their relationship with you. This means considering not only what the neighborhood looks like and what it says about your business, but also whether your location is easy to reach.

Home Sweet Office

If you decide to have a homebased office, you can locate it anywhere in your home that works for you. Take a look at the worksheet we have given you on page 32 to help you with these decisions. Several of the personal concierges we talked to started out with home businesses. One located her office in the basement, another set hers up in a spare bedroom, and another was lucky enough to have a large room in her home designed to be an office.

Some people locate their office in a den, garage, corner of the kitchen or dining room, or even in a closet! Sure, that option wouldn't work for long if your business grew rapidly or if you had a need for employees. But in the beginning, if you had nowhere else to put your computer, you could clear out a closet, turn a box upside down, set up your computer, and go to work. The best thing about it is that nobody ever has to know your office is in a closet because when com-pany comes over, all you have to do is shut the door—and voilà! the office is hidden.

No Need for the Tax Man Blues

Some personal concierges will tell you there is one great advantage to having a home-based business: You can write some expenses off your income taxes. If you are using even a portion of your home for an office, the IRS

Tip...

Smart Tip

If you decide to have a home office, you'll probably want to set some ground rules for friends and family. Make sure they realize that just because you're working from home, you're not available to run errands for them during the day or to baby-sit on a moment's notice. Let them know that during working hours, you're working! They'll respect you for being upfront, and you'll be able to focus on your job.

will allow you to write off some costs as a home business deduction. You are allowed to claim that deduction if—and only if—you are using that space solely for an office. If you're using the space for other things as well, you can't claim it as a deduction. You can get information from the IRS about tax deductions for homebased businesses by visiting www.irs.gov.

Rules and Regulations

You'll need to learn about your local zoning regulations if you decide to locate your office in your home. The personal concierge business isn't the type of business in which you'd have clients visiting your office, so you should not have to worry about parking restrictions or annoyed neighbors. But you should still make a call to your local county clerk's office and ask whether any permits are needed.

While you're on the phone, go ahead and inquire about a business license, if you haven't already. Since you've come this far, you want to make sure you have all of your t's crossed and your i's dotted.

Growth Spurt

You may find that you eventually have to make the jump from a homebased business to an office away from home. Although many of the personal concierges we interviewed did indeed have home businesses, others who had started at home had been forced to move when their businesses began growing.

One of the concierges we talked to had started her business in a corner of her dining room; another located hers in a spare bedroom. Larissa Erven of Ms. Errands notes,

Caller ID is your friend

Use technology to your advantage especially when you're working from home. If you have a single phone line for home and your business when you're starting out, make sure you get a phone service package that includes Caller ID and voice mail with Caller ID. You can be on the phone with a your child's teacher and see that the call coming in is a client, then make the choice of whom to talk to at that particular moment. You can also skip calls (like from your utility or credit card company offering you the latest fraud protection) during your workday that you can attend to after hours. It's not about screening calls, but using technology to prioritize your calls to make the most of your time. Plus with voice mail, callers always get your voice mail, never a busy signal.

Change of Heart

When Katharine G., from Raleigh, North Carolina, decided to start her personal concierge business, she knew her business would not be home-based. "I used to have an event-planning business," she says. "I ran the business out of my basement and for a variety of reasons, the business just was not working. It wasn't going well at all."

This time, Katharine spent considerable time researching different locations and ended up with office space in a corporate building. Because her business has employees, she needed a larger office than she could find at home anyway.

She says concierges who are looking for office space should leave no stone unturned. "Talk to everyone you know because they might have a friend of a friend of a friend who is about to move out of their office space and it could be just the right office for you."

"The only downfall to [working from home] is you have to be really disciplined. It's really easy to fall in a rut and get 'lazy' or distracted, especially in the building phase of your business. I would highly recommend starting out of your home if at all possible, as long as you can stay focused on work. It will save you a lot in overhead expenses in the long run." Ida S. still runs her business from home saying she'll continue to do so, "until my staff grows beyond three, whereupon I will move the business to an offsite office." She provides this excellent reminder, "A home office must be completely separate from the living quarters." Loreine G. points out two things to consider before running your business from home, "Prepare yourself for a complete lack of structure. There is no boss to tell you when to get up, so it is imperative that you treat your home office like any other office and maintain a disciplined schedule. Also, it's very easy to become a hermit when you when you work from home, so it is important to delegate what work you can do so you can maintain community ties as the business owner.

When you think about it, a homebased business can quickly take over your life in terms of paperwork, files, phone calls at all hours, FedEx deliveries on a daily basis, faxes, mail, etc.

If you do decide to start looking for an office away from home, the options are endless. You can look into sharing an office with another businessperson or check out corporate office spaces that may be underutilized and are offering good deals on rent. You can also check

Tip...

Smart Tip

One call—or sometimes two—can do it all. Just call the state and local government offices in your area to find out what permits are required for your business.

Home Office Location Worksheet

Use this handy worksheet to pick the best place in your home for an office.
Name four possible office locations in your home.

1. _____

2. _____

3. _____

4. _____

Make a list of the pros and cons of each location.

1. What is the lighting situation? Do you think you'd have adequate lighting? If not, can anything be done to change that?

   _____

   _____

   _____

2. Is there room to set up your computer and any other supplies you might need?

   _____

   _____

   _____

3. What about noise? Will you be able to concentrate or are you right next to a window where you'd have to listen to a leaf blower for an hour every morning?

   _____

   _____

   _____

4. Are there adequate phone and electrical outlets? How frustrating to get everything set up and then realize you don't have phone or electrical outlets within reach.

   _____

   _____

   _____

out other options, including renting a house or an apartment for your business. Remember, what you need is space and not a fancy address since, more than likely, your clients won't visit your office very often—if ever.

Some entrepreneurs lease space over storefronts. If you do find such a space, make sure the storefront is one you won't mind sharing space with and not one that could hurt your image. Some concierges report having very good luck locating their offices in business parks or busy corporate areas because of the networking possibilities. None of them seemed too hip on locating their offices near busy shopping centers, though, because these places lacked the business image they were aiming to project.

But you can decide on these issues for yourself because every town and city is different, and what works for one person might not work for you. By the same token, what didn't work for someone else might work perfectly for you!

We've covered all of the important factors involved in laying the groundwork for your business. The structures, fees, and licenses mentioned should be the main ones you'll have to consider. The more information you have, the better prepared you will be for your new business venture. And you can never have too much good information.

Money Is No
Obstacle

In this chapter, we come face to face with the costs involved in starting a personal concierge service. Don't worry, it's not as scary as it sounds. We've provided a list of items you need to properly equip your office, and we've given a rundown of the operating expenses you can expect to encounter. You'll find sample worksheets for figuring your start-up costs as well as your monthly income and operating expenses. With a little ingenuity, you won't have to break the bank.

Start-Up Costs

It's time to get down to the nitty-gritty of just how much it costs to get your business up and running. One of the best things about establishing a personal concierge business is that the start-up costs can be minimal. That benefit is one we heard about over and over again from personal concierges. The low start-up costs were one of the things that attracted them to the business in the first place. Many started running their business from home with around $500 and equipment they already had, like computers and telephones.

Since you won't have to purchase inventory, your biggest expenses aside from office equipment will be for advertising, business cards, stationery, and web site design.

Here's a rundown of what you'll need to get your business off to a roaring start:

- A good computer system with a modem, CD or DVD burner, and printer
- Software for accounting and contact management
- Fax machine or service
- Scanner (consider an all-in-one device printer/fax/scanner)
- Phone with two or three lines and caller ID
- Answering machine or voice mail
- Cellular phone (preferably a Smartphone with e-mail capability, like a Treo or Blackberry, for example)
- Personal Digital Assistant (PDA) like a Palm device
- Office supplies and stationery, including business cards
- High speed internet access (like DSL, cable, or satellite)
- Web site (including hosting, design, and implementation)
- Insurance
- Legal and accounting services
- Start-up advertising

You may already have most of the basic office equipment. Of course, if you're one of those lucky people for whom money is no object, you can add all sorts of extras to

Bright Idea

Cynthia A., the personal concierge in San Diego, says even when she's not at work, she's often thinking about work—and about her clients. "If I'm driving and I spot a new restaurant, entertainment venue, bakery, or something like that, I always make note of it because it might be useful in the future," she says. "I'm constantly asking questions and thinking about the marketing of my business."

your office: file cabinets, bookshelves, comfortable chairs, a copier, and anything else your heart desires. We've provided a checklist of equipment you'll need to get up and running on page 48.

If you're like most folks starting a new business, you are really watching your budget and don't want to spend a penny more than you have to. If you're really scrimping, you can find many ways to cut corners. Remember, your clients never have to see your home office, so if you don't have the funds to buy a computer desk, no problem! Set up the computer on your kitchen counter or dining room table. Do your best to keep it as separate as possible from the rest of your home to stay as productive as possible.

Getting Equipped

Start-up expenses for your business will vary depending on factors such as your office location, how much equipment you need to buy, and how much start-up capital you have at your disposal. (See the worksheet on page 40 for examples). Use the worksheet on page 41 to come up with your own official start-up figure.

Computer Choices

You and your computer are going to be spending a lot of time together, for everything from keeping track of your clients' requests to generating invoices and taking care of accounting. So, you need to find a computer that can meet the needs of your business. How do you decide which is the best one for you? Research what's out there by reading product reviews and talking to computer experts, then do some comparison shopping.

Choose from two basic operating systems, Windows and Mac. Both systems have their critics and their proponents, so if you already have a favorite, feel free to stick with it. If you're starting from scratch, consider getting a Windows-based machine, because most of the software being developed in the industry is written for Windows.

To be able to take full advantage of internet capabilities, as well as store files and run various programs, you should make sure that your computer has at least 1 GB processor, 1GB to 2MB RAM, plus at least a 60GB hard drive and a CD/DVD drive. You should also make sure you have an Ethernet port and several USB connections to install peripherals, like your printer, scanner, speakers, flash drives and a camera.

Be prepared to pay from $800 to $2,000 for a good computer system, including the printer.

Smart Tip

Tip...

Before you go computer shopping, jot down a short list of what you want your system to do. It will save you some time and make your trek to the computer store a lot easier.

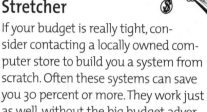

Dollar Stretcher

If your budget is really tight, consider contacting a locally owned computer store to build you a system from scratch. Often these systems can save you 30 percent or more. They work just as well, without the big budget advertising and branded stickers on the side. Plus you know who to take it to if you have any trouble.

Remember, a desktop machine will be cheaper than a laptop or notebook computer with the same system specifications. Don't forget to check out sales at local stores like Best Buy, CompUSA, and Circuit City, warehouse stores like Sam's Club and Costco, and directly from the manufacturer like Dell.com, Apple.com, or Gateway.com. Shop around and look for discounts; it can make a big difference to your pocketbook, especially when you're starting a new business and every penny counts. But don't panic if you don't have this much extra money on hand. You can stick with the computer you have or buy a simple system for now and upgrade later. Choose a high-powered desktop now and add a middle-of-the-road laptop later, for example.

Flashing Your Clients

What is a USB flash drive? Well, basically, it's a device that allows you to quickly copy material from your hard drive onto a portable disk drive. Why do you need a USB flash drive? Consider this: You've just updated your computer files, which now include information on 30 potential clients, some recent market-research data, and a couple of files you plan to use in a new promotional brochure. What happens if your computer

A Word about Wireless

Wireless computing devices are already as commonplace today as cell phones were 10 years ago, and that shows no sign of stopping anytime soon. If you can afford to buy a laptop, do so, especially if you have a home office. Make sure that it has a wireless modem built in. You can conduct business meetings with full access to your files at a client's office, at a hotel, or wherever you need to. Many public places have free wireless internet access for their customers. You can meet a client at one of several nationally known restaurants (like Starbucks, Panera Bread, or McDonalds). Most hotels also have wireless internet access on their property, which is great if you're onsite planning an event and need to access the internet or send a quick e-mail. Once you have a computer with wireless internet access, you'll be surprised you lived without it.

Book It!

Make sure your brain is as well-equipped as your office. When it comes to checking out the written word regarding your new business venture, you should plan on becoming a real bookworm. Visit bookstores and libraries and take a look at online bookstores. There is a listing of helpful books in the Appendix at the back of this book, but here are a few more titles you may want to get your hands on.

- ○ *Thank You Very Much: A Book for Anyone Who Has Ever Said, "May I Help You?"* (Ten Speed Press), by Holly Stiel
- ○ *The Guerilla Marketing Handbook* (Houghton Mifflin Co.), by Jay Conrad Levinson and Seth Godin
- ○ *Start Your Own Business*, (Entrepreneur Press) by Rieva Lesonsky
- ○ *Business as Unusual* (Anita Roddick Books) by Anita Roddick
- ○ *Anyone Can Do It* (Capstone) by Sahar & Bobby Hashemi
- ○ *Kickstart Marketing* (Allen & Unwin Pty., Limited (Australia)) by Linda Hailey
- ○ *Organizing from the Inside Out* (Owl Books) by Julie Morgenstern

Don't wait for a rainy day to curl up in bed with a good book or two. Get all your errands and personal business out of the way during the week, and plan to devote a Saturday to catching up on your reading.

If the weather is cool, make a cup of hot chocolate, settle back with your books, and start reading! All that studying will pay off as you fire up your business because you'll be equipped with everything you learned in those written pages.

crashes or gets stolen? The answer is simple but frightening: You would lose all of that hard work. But if you have a USB flash drive, you can copy important files onto it and store the drive in a separate place. That way, if something happens to your computer, you'll have a solid backup.

They range in size from 32 MB up to 64 GB. You can obtain a 1 to 4 GB USB flash drive for $25-40. The cost for backing up your company data, priceless. Keep an extra on hand for taking proposals from your computer to the print shop quickly and easily.

The Software Scene

Most of the personal concierges we talked to say that they don't need fancy software programs because their work mostly involves dealing with clients one-on-one, tracking down hard-to-find items, or making arrangements by phone. However, some

Start-Up Expenses

Here's a list of start-up expenses for two hypothetical personal concierge services. The first is a one-person, homebased business called ACE Concierge. The business owner already has a personal computer and some of the basic office equipment he will need. First Class Concierge, on the other hand, is based out of a commercial office space, and has one full-time employee. The owner of First Class decided to invest in a new computer system, a deluxe web site, and a large initial advertising campaign. Neither owner draws a salary; instead, they take a percentage of their net profits as income.

Expenses	ACE	First Class
Rent & utilities (deposit and first month)	N/A	$1,700
Office equipment and supplies	$750	$3,000
Phone system (including voice mail and cell phone)	$200	$300
Employee payroll & benefits	N/A	$1,800
Licenses	$150	$150
Insurance (first six months)	$500	$1,000
Internet access (modem and first month)	$150	$600
Web site design	$300	$4,000
Legal and accounting services	$150	$500
Start-up advertising	$500	$1,000
Rolodex or little black book	(Priceless)	(Priceless)
Memberships	$500	$5,000
Miscellaneous (add 10% of Total)	$320	$1,905
Total Start-Up Costs	**$3,520**	**$20,955**

of them did splurge on accounting software programs. Others took the plunge and purchased software programs specifically designed for payroll concerns. But if you are going to operate a one-person, homebased business, you won't have to deal with payroll issues and your accounting concerns will be minimal.

Still, software programs abound, and since you are going to be shopping for computers, printers, fax machines, etc., you might as well take a look at the software, too. You might come across the perfect piece of software to make your day-to-day business life easier. Most personal concierges use Intuit QuickBooks, Quicken, or similar programs

Start-Up Expenses Worksheet

Use this worksheet to calculate your own start-up costs. If you decide on a homebased office, you won't need to worry about rent or employee expenses.

Expenses

Rent and utilities (deposit and first month)	$_____
Office equipment and supplies	_____
Phone system (including voice mail and cell phone)	_____
Employee payroll and benefits	_____
Licenses	_____
Insurance (first six months)	_____
Internet access	_____
Web site design	_____
Legal and accounting services	_____
Start-up advertising	_____
Miscellaneous (add 10% of Total)	_____
Official Start-Up Figure	$_____

for keeping track of finances and generating invoices. Others find someone to take care of those needs for them. For your own business, it will depend on how big a client list you have and whether you can find a software program that keeps you from drowning in financial paperwork.

Internet Access

Every concierge we interviewed had internet access and reported that it was vital for several reasons. For starters, it allows one more avenue to keep in touch—via e-mail. With internet access, you can send and receive e-mail from clients, fellow concierges, other business contacts, and vendors. You can research hotels, read restaurant reviews,

▲

Dollar Stretcher

Many companies purchase USB flash drives in bulk, slap their logo on them, load them up with product documentation, and ship them off to individual clients. If you're lucky enough to receive one of these giveaways, don't simply toss it once you've read the marketing material. Instead, dump the files and use the drive for your own purposes.

order film processing, send grocery orders to the market, and schedule appointments. Internet access also opens up a whole world of research possibilities for the business owner. Information on every topic you could possibly imagine is available with the click of a mouse. Check out the Appendix for information on great online groups for the aspiring personal concierge.

The cost of internet access is surprisingly low. We recommend using a high speed internet connection like DSL or cable. The monthly service is surprising affordable, with rates starting as low as $12.95. Both high speed connections require a special modem to process the signal coming into your home, then connect to your computer. In most cases, the company will give you the modem for free. If they don't offer it, ask. Contact your phone company, satellite TV, or cable TV provider for services and prices in your area.

If high speed connections aren't available in your area, a slightly cheaper, but much less effective, option is to choose a dial-up ISP (Internet Service Provider) like PeoplePC, NetZero, or ATT Yahoo! Dial-up Service. It works anywhere you can find a phone line, but it works slowly. As more sites on the internet take advantage of graphic-intensive applications, dial-up will not be able to keep up. Basic programs start at $5.95 a month. Even though it's dirt cheap, we highly recommend using a high speed connection for just a few bucks more. It will save you so much time, and free up your phone line for calls!

Web Site

Most of the concierges we talked to cite their web sites as the number one resource for gaining new clients. The others note that referrals from satisfied clients was number one with a web site as a very close number two. "My clients are nationwide. The non-local clients are serviced by a member of the Concierges Connection in their location," says Ida S., the personal concierge based near Cleveland, Ohio. Kathy S., the personal concierge in Elkhart, Indiana, once planned a wedding in Carmel, California. The world is truly getting smaller!

Designing Your Web Site

Some concierges create their own web sites and others hire designers. Ultimately, the choice is up to you. You have to look at your own computer skills, budget, and image you're looking to portray and decide what works. The concierges who hired site designers to build their sites were all happy with their decision. All they had to do was supply the information they wanted to include in their sites. Sites can be very simple, just one page giving the company's name, address, and phone number; or they can include multiple pages with photos and even music, as well as basic business information. It's wise to do your research on this one and get recommendations from your friends or other business owners who have had their web sites designed. Also, look at sites to see what features you like and don't like. If you see a site you really like, look at the bottom of the page, it will usually have the name of the designer and contact information.

Costs of having a web site built for you vary widely depending on what type of site you want, how in demand the designer is, and what type of experience he or she has. Calling a few places at random, we found that costs could be anywhere from $199 to several thousand dollars. We talked to one web designer who said a client had paid him $12,000 to design a site with multiple pages, tons of photos, and music on each page. Although it cost a pretty penny, the site was a beauty, the designer said. Keep in mind that you can start on the low end, with a web site offering just your basic business information, and add the bells and whistles later.

Hosting Your Web Site

You can have all the content created for your web site, but you have to actually put it up on the internet before anyone can see it. You can find a slew of companies that host your nonbusiness personal webpage for free. But since you are running a business, you will likely have to pay to have your site hosted. Many companies, Yahoo! Small Business or GoDaddy.com, are geared perfectly for small business users to quickly and affordably register their web site address, host their web site, create the pages, and even manage online marketing campaigns with a one-stop shop. Prices start at around $10 a month (or lower if you buy a year at a time) for the most basic services.

The Fine Print

New printer models are coming out every day, and there are some great choices out there. You can find a decent inkjet printer for under $150. But if you plan to design your own brochures and marketing materials, you might consider a laser printer in the $500 range.

Again, you'll want to shop around. And don't forget to factor in the cost of ink. A single inkjet print cartridge can run between $20 and $40, so if you do a lot of printing it can definitely add up.

Many different companies offer printing services, so don't feel like you have to splurge on an expensive printer right away. FedEx Kinkos (www.fedex.com) allows you to print right from your word processing program (like Microsoft Word) directly to a store near you, with its File, Print, FedEx Kinko's software. In fact, if you're shipping the item you're printing, they can do it all for you while you sit in your cozy

Dollar Stretcher

You're probably going to be purchasing printer/copier/fax paper in bulk, so make sure to ask the store you patronize if you can get a discount. Most store owners will be more than happy to do so because it guarantees a repeat customer who may spread the word about the store's policy.

office. No need to even physically deliver the file to them.

Just the Fax

Sure, you can get by without a fax machine or service. But it would probably be to your advantage to have one because your clients will really appreciate it. Say you're working on getting some price quotes for a cruise for one client and running down costs for a 50th anniversary party for another client. Instead of putting the quotes in the mail or leaving the info on an answering machine, you could just fax the information to your clients, guaranteeing that they would have it in minutes. Saving time and money on postage.

These days a big clunky fax machine may seem like a relic (or at a minimum, an expensive door stop). But just a few short years ago, most business (even those which were homebased) had a fax machine. Today, you have another option a fax service. You can create documents on your computer, then send them to a client's fax machine (or their fax service) instantly. If they have a traditional fax machine,

they'll receive the hard copy, black and white document they expect to see, never suspecting that you "faxed" it virtually. If they have a service, they can likely view their document on their computer then print it as they wish. Check out a service like eFax (www.efax.com) that has a basic free (yes, I said free) service to get you started. And if you're looking for the ability to edit and manipulate the text in the faxes you receive, take a look at its eFax Pro service for a small monthly fee.

If you choose to go the route of freestanding fax machine rather than service, we recommend a combination unit that's a fax/copier/printer/scanner. Again, plan to shop around and take your time finding just the right machine for you. Prices range from $200 to $600 for multifunction fax machines.

Dollar Stretcher

Don't be too quick to buy a freestanding fax machine. If you're using a suite of office productivity software (meaning programs with word processing, spreadsheet, and database programs like Microsoft Office), you likely can set your system up to fax directly from your documents. Look in your Help information to see the steps that work for your system. In Microsoft Word 2007, for example, click on the Office icon in the upper left-hand corner, select "Send," and choose the "Internet Fax" option to try out a service.

Line One Is for You

We'll just take it for granted that you already have a phone line in your home. But if you're going to base your business at home, it really is necessary to go ahead and get a second line. Why? The best scenario is to have one line for personal use and a second line for business use. If you insist on having an actual fax machine, consider getting a third line specifically for it. (Saving money by not getting a third line, it's just one more reason to use a fax service.)

Dollar Stretcher

Why pay a long-distance fee if you can call your vendors on their toll-free number? When a vendor signs a contract, make it a point to ask if the company has a toll-free number. The savings add up!

It's also a good idea to have a two-line phone for your business so you can put one caller on hold while you answer a second line. This way, if you're on the phone and a call is coming in, you won't miss that important call you've been waiting for.

Some entrepreneurs like to have speakerphones so they can attend to other things while talking to their clients. But be forewarned that some people don't like their calls being broadcast on speakerphones. If you plan to use a speakerphone while talking to clients, ask them ahead of time if it's OK. A good speakerphone, equipped with two lines, auto redial, mute button, memory dial, and other features, ranges from about $75 to $150. Shop around and look for sales and other specials, and you can sometimes get a better deal.

Concierges with a lot of out-of-town clients say toll-free numbers are a must for them so their clients can always get in touch with them without any long distance charges. Those concierges who serve mostly in-town clients don't see a need for a toll-free number. This is one more case where you will need to make that decision based on your business, your volume of calls, and whether you have a lot of out-of-town clients.

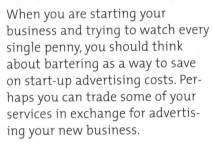

Dollar Stretcher

When you are starting your business and trying to watch every single penny, you should think about bartering as a way to save on start-up advertising costs. Perhaps you can trade some of your services in exchange for advertising your new business.

Don't Miss a Call

It's important to make sure you receive all of your incoming calls even if you aren't there to take them yourself. To make sure you get all your messages, you'll need to have either an answering machine or voice mail. We recommend voice mail, so every call is answered and clients never get a busy signal. And if some natural disaster strikes and you find yourself without power, your voice mail may still work, while an answering machine likely won't.

Smart Tip

Find out if the phone company you're using offers features like call forwarding. You can forward your business line to your cell phone, so you never miss a call while you're on the go.

Just like an answering machine, voice mail takes your messages when you can't be in the office. Voice mail costs vary depending on which features you choose, but basic voice mail service from your local phone company generally runs in the neighborhood of $6 to $10 per month.

Whatever you do, make sure you have something in place to handle those all-important calls that are sure to come in the second you step out of the office. The worst thing that can happen when a client calls you is for the phone to just ring and ring. If clients get that kind of reception on their first call, they might never make a second call. You don't want that to happen! With a new business, every client counts. Try to avoid using a cutesy script on your answering machine or voice-mail message. These will only make you look unprofessional.

For a basic two-line speaker phone with caller ID, expect to pay between $60 and $100; for a fancier model, you'll spend anywhere from $150 to $200.

Cellular Phones and Other Gadgets

Every concierge we talked to said they wouldn't dream of being without their cellular phone. Sure, your clients can leave a message on your answering machine or send you an e-mail. But what about those clients who want something handled yesterday? If they can't reach you, they may turn to someone else.

With the increase in popularity of cellular phones, most companies are literally giving phones away with a two-year service agreement. Full functioning smartphones, like the Blackberry or the Treo, will set you back $200–$300 with a two-year service agreement. With a smartphone you have instant access to receive and send e-mail from anywhere you have a phone service. Most smartphones allow you the ability to make and receive phone calls, conduct internet searches, manage your schedule, manage e-mail, use some office software (like viewing and editing documents and spreadsheets), take photos and video, record voice memos, and listen to music, all from a single device.

Smart Tip

If you're looking for an upgrade to standard voicemail, consider using a virtual receptionist service like eVoice Receptionist. eVoice answers the phone when you can't, transfers them to one of your extensions (home, business, cell, as you see fit), then sends voicemails to you as e-mail attachments. All for the low price of $29.95 a month.

For a professional who needs to be ready at all times to fill a need, it's not a luxury, it's a necessity.

If you choose not to get a smartphone, make sure you keep a PDA (or personal digital assistant) that you can quickly synchronize with your computer, to keep your schedule at your fingertips wherever you go.

The expense of a cellular phone can vary widely depending on usage and your service plan. For instance, if you talk in the neighborhood of 450 minutes a month (or around 15 minutes a day), you could pay as little as $40 per month, but if you talk 6000 minutes a month (roughly 3 hours a day), you might spend $70 per month. If you add a data package to get e-mail, it's around an additional $40 per month. Make sure you read the fine print. Many companies allow you to talk to their other customers for free, not using any minutes out of your pool of minutes, or they let you choose five to ten numbers to call for free. There are literally hundreds of options, so look for the plan that fits you and your business best.

Getting Your Name Out

Every concierge we interviewed emphasized the importance of having business stationery because it creates the professional image you want your clients to have of you and your new business. What exactly do you need when it comes to stationery? For starters, you should have business cards, letterhead, and envelopes.

Since this is one of the few real expenses you'll incur, you really shouldn't cut corners here. But, you can shop around. Look at your local print shop and online resources as well. VistaPrint.com has a wide variety of both free and premium business cards at reasonable prices. GotPrint is another competitively priced internet option. And OvernightPrints.com promises a 24-hour turnaround on most jobs.

Start-Up Advertising

We will discuss advertising more in Chapter 6, but we want to give you an idea of how much some concierges spent on advertising when they launched their businesses. One concierge designed and wrote all the copy for her brochure and incurred only the cost of printing and mailing, a sum of about $250.

Another concierge bought newspaper ads, had fliers made up, and also mailed some materials to potential clients. She spent approximately $1,000 on her initial ad campaign.

Yet another concierge advertised mostly by word-of-mouth and by tacking self-designed fliers on bulletin boards around town. She estimates she spent about $50 on her complete campaign.

Equipment Checklist

You can use this checklist as a guide for equipping your office. This list is not carved in stone, and it may contain more (or fewer) items than you need for your office. Look it over, add to it, and make changes as needed.

❑ Computer $\$$ _____

❑ USB flash drive _____

❑ Printer/scanner combination _____

❑ Office productivity software _____

❑ Accounting software _____

❑ Contact management software _____

❑ Phone system (two or three lines) _____

❑ Voice mail or answering machine _____

❑ PDA _____

❑ Cellular phone _____

❑ Surge protector _____

❑ Calculator _____

❑ Extra printer cartridge _____

❑ Internet modem _____

❑ Printer/copier/fax paper _____

❑ Letterhead stationery/business cards _____

❑ Miscellaneous office supplies _____

You can decide what's right for you and how much money you can afford to spend. But if you have no clients at all, a large ad campaign might be a wise place to start.

Getting Coverage

Since the first edition of this book came out, insurance companies have begun to acknowledge the concierge industry and work toward developing a proper category for it. The ICEA reports that a few carriers, like American Family and Wheaton Insurance, have created a special Errands and Shopping category for writing insurance policies. But many concierges complain that their maximum coverage isn't high enough for the potential lawsuits they might incur. Most experts agree that you should choose an amount of coverage as least as great as the amount that someone could sue you for. And try going through an independent insurance agent that sells policies from many different companies. She may know of just the answer for getting you coverage in your area.

Several insurance representatives told us that, unless you have employees, you shouldn't need any special coverage. If you do have employees, you'll want to check into workers' compensation coverage, which can cost around $500 to $3,000 per year but can vary widely depending on where you live. If you're transporting people during the course of your business, the cost could go up substantially. You'll also want to make sure your employees are fully insured if they are going to be driving for your company. And every concierge we talked to who had employees purchased Employee Dishonesty Bonds. These bonds protect you, the business owner, from liability in the event your employees commit dishonest acts while performing their duties.

Most concierges said it is important to at least have general liability insurance, although they all reported some confusion when their insurance company attempted to categorize their business. According to the personal concierges we interviewed, there is no specific "concierge" category within insurance companies. Some concierges have even found their insurance carriers were classifying them under "limousine companies" because there was no specific category for them. As the concierge business continues to grow, expect to see the industry get its own category. In the meantime, you can still get liability insurance as a business owner.

Legal and Accounting Services

As we've mentioned, it's always wise to consult an attorney if you have legal questions pertaining to your business. If you are going to set up a partnership or corporation, you will definitely need an attorney because certain legal documents have to be filed, and you'll need an attorney's expertise for that. This is another area in which expenses can vary widely depending on what area of the country you live in as well as

▲

Smart Tip

Tip...

Did you know that the IRS has all sorts of business publications available for the business owner? And they're free! Check out its web site at www.irs.gov or give it a call at (800) TAX-FORM.

how much of the attorney's time you take up. Most attorneys charge by the hour; although some offer free consultations, others charge $100 or more for an hour-long consultation. Call around and also ask friends or other business owners to refer you to a good lawyer.

Don't be afraid to barter your services for legal and financial advice. Jennifer C. of Gainesville, Georgia, got to know an attorney through her chamber of commerce. She told him about her business, and after talking a bit, she asked him to review some of her contracts. He agreed to look at them and give his advice in exchange for her picking up his dry cleaning for an agreed upon period. He loved the service so much, she kept him as a client even after the legal work was completed.

Some personal concierges have used legal services, like Pre-paid Legal Services (www.prepaidlegal.com), paying a small set amount each month to have unlimited contact with an attorney via the telephone during regular business hours. They can also review documents and contracts for you, send letters to help settle disputes, and even represent you at trial, all for a flat fee.

Is It Raining Money?

Even though getting a personal concierge service up and running costs relatively little, it still takes a bit of money, especially if you don't already have a good computer, cell phone, and other necessary equipment. So, where should the money come from? Some personal concierges use their savings; others take out loans; and still others borrow from family or friends. And there are also many other avenues.

Jennifer C. used money she received in a settlement after an automobile accident to start her business. Another concierge shared, "I originally looked into a small business loan but after realizing that the majority of banks wanted you to be in business for three years, or have a substantial amount of equity or assets to use as collateral, I decided not to apply. I had some money left over from refinancing my house and that is what I used."

Since the amount of money required to get a concierge business up and running is relatively small, most concierges said if you are short on capital the best way to get funds is to look for a loan from family members or friends. Generally, unless you need a considerable amount of capital, you shouldn't need to seek out a traditional loan.

Getting Help

As the number of personal concierge businesses grows, companies are emerging that will, for a fee, set up entrepreneurs in their own personal concierge businesses. It's a bit different from franchising in that most companies charge only a one-time fee, and after getting new concierges on their feet, leave them on their own. Go to your favorite search engine and type in "Start a personal concierge business" and look at all the pretty links.

One company in particular looks helpful to the concierge just getting started, Concierges Connection based out of the Cleveland area. It's launching a new service in the summer of 2007 that provides a turnkey solution to starting your personal concierge business. Ida Stanley, owner of Concierges Connection, says, "offerings are online solutions available 24/7 that offer the necessary tools to operate their business that new and established concierge services will benefit from." Her company is developing a set of online tools that help a concierge do everything, including setting up a CRM (customer relationship management) database, running a day-to-day business, creating marketing materials, and designing and hosting a web site. It's developing online training modules to minimize the amount of time and money spent on travelling to and from training sites. Ida gave an idea of the kinds of training modules in development, saying, "Among others we are creating Best Practices (a How to Series that includes the very basics for both starting and expanding your concierge business), the Pricing Workshop (Selling at the Right Price), and Closing the Sale."

There are also a few concierge consultants out there who specialize in helping entrepreneurs get businesses up and running. Triangle Concierge offers consulting services dealing with everything from sample contracts for concierges to a business plan. Its site also offers a concierge bookstore, where potential concierges can get info on vendors, meeting and event planning, and much more. Angel At Your Service offers many different products for running your concierge business. It's also developing a travelling seminar, called Errand and Concierge Service University to teach the industry basics. You'll find details in the Appendix on how to contact all of the concierges we interviewed for this book. But do your own research, too. Kellye G. found the perfect answer for her training needs, "I contacted a concierge doing business in Austin and asked to pay her a consulting fee to help me. I drove to Austin to meet her."

Concierge consultants have certainly found a niche. Some reportedly charge between $800 to $2000 per person for a three-day seminar on the basics of getting a personal concierge company up and running. Put your calculator to those numbers and it doesn't take long to figure out why someone created that niche.

So What Do You Do?
Daily Operations

Now we're going to tackle the daily ins and outs of running a personal concierge business, and although that might sound very buttoned-up and serious, this will be a fun chapter. You'll hear about a typical day in the life of a concierge and some of the requests—both the exotic and mundane—that personal concierges have received. You will find out how concierges handle billing and also learn some valuable customer service tips.

Putting in the Hours

One of the best things about the life of an entrepreneur is that you set your own schedule. If you're not a morning person and you don't have to see clients first thing in the morning, then you don't even have to set an alarm. But come 2 P.M., you might find yourself working like a maniac, especially if you're the type of person who hits your high-energy peak in the afternoon. The point is, you can decide what kind of hours you want to work and how you want to structure your work hours, as long as you can meet your clients' needs.

And keep in mind, if you do work odd hours from a home office, your clients don't ever have to know your work habits or even that you work from home. With today's technology, you'll likely be communicating via e-mail, voice mail, or fax. If there is a need for a face-to-face meeting with a client, you can always set up a business lunch.

A Day in the Life

Wondering what a regular workday might be like once you get your business off the ground? Of course, "regular" means different things to different people. Many variables may affect your day, such as whether you have a home office or an office away from home, whether you work full time or part time, and whether you serve mostly corporate clients or mostly personal clients.

Loreine G. says she typically wakes up "around 6 A.M. to work out, shower, and dress. I hit the computer and make the errand schedule for the day, which an employee will take at 9 A.M. I usually man the computer until 7 P.M. when there is typically some event to go to, and then I come home and continue to work until around 10 P.M." Abbie Martin, a concierge in Australia, describes her day like a to-do list, "Work for a client in their office on administration and marketing tasks. Visit clients' homes to water garden or let in cleaner/tradesperson. Order gift/flowers on behalf of clients. Grocery shopping for another clients. Phone calls to coordinate tradespeople/new suppliers for my clients." A busy girl indeed! Kathy S. looks at her week to describe the regular schedule of her business, "During the week I make several visits to people's homes for pet sitting duties. Generally, I have one weekly shopping trip for clients. I try to group my requests together to save on trips. I make at least one trip to the mall or specialty store. I spend the rest of the time answering questions, doing marketing, returning e-mails, and attending networking events. I also find time to do longer term projects like research invitations for a wedding I'm planning." The day we spoke with her she also packed in an appearance on a local radio show and a luncheon talk geared toward make Valentine's Day special at her local Elks club.

Larissa E. echoes the sentiments of most of the concierges we interviewed, "That's the great part—no two days are the same. Some days are really busy from start to finish, and others are pretty slow. Some days I feel like I'm on the phone or computer all day and others I'm busy running around like a chicken with its head cut off." The one thing they know they will be doing every day is juggling many tasks, and they must be prepared to do that. Some of them carry smartphones, PDAs, or other similar task-management gadgets while they are on the go. Others use filing systems or databases in the office.

Bright Idea

If you have a cell phone or PDA, it may have a voice recorder feature built right in. Use it to jot down or record your thoughts when you see something that might benefit your business. The tape recorder is handy when you're driving and can't write down notes. If you drive past a new restaurant or florist, you can record the name and any other information and follow up on it later. And it never hurts to keep a pen and paper handy!

When asked how many projects they might take on in an average day, some of the personal concierges said there were too many to count; others, who had smaller operations, said their best guess would be dozens. Concierges say it's difficult to estimate how many tasks they perform because some of their duties are so routine, such as calling clients or vendors, checking e-mail, etc. But make no mistake, most concierges are high-energy, incredibly busy people who virtually never sit still during their workday.

Concierges also say no two clients are the same. Some clients call and want something done yesterday; others generally give the concierge some notice. But as a rule, most concierges say they receive lots of last-minute requests. "It can definitely throw a wrench in things if you're going in one direction and have to change your pace," Cynthia says. "But it's also par for the course, and it's one of the things I enjoy about my work—the unknown."

Beware!

Are you a self-starter? Are you disciplined? If not, you'd better learn something about those traits quickly—especially if you're planning to run a homebased business. If you spend your days goofing off, there won't be any checks showing up in your mailbox.

Making Fantasies Come True

Cynthia tells of a client whose daughter wanted to see pop superstar Ricky Martin in concert. The only problem was that the concert had been sold out for weeks. But the client

Sure, as Long as It's Legal

We asked concierges all over the United States to give us some of the most unusual requests they had received from clients. In most of these cases, the concierge was able to come through for the client.

○ *Ox gallstones.* After spending considerable time on the phone, a concierge informed a client that ox gallstones were available at a slaughterhouse for $1,000 per ounce. The client decided he didn't want them that badly. The concierge later learned that ox gallstones are sometimes thought to be an aphrodisiac.

○ *Arranging a wedding ceremony on the front steps of a nationally known museum located in Cleveland with only three days notice.*

○ *Move a playhouse from one backyard to another.*

○ *Pick up a pet dog from the pound after he had escaped.*

○ *Physically go wake up a hung-over employee, get them showered, and to work.*

○ *Complete a purse exchange.* Two sets of grandparents were visiting their kids during a holiday and the respective grannies left for home with the other's purse. The concierge had to do a purse exchange at 11 P.M. on a Sunday night because one set of grandparents was flying out the next morning.

○ *Catch two cats who may or may not bring dead things along with them.* One concierges had a client that had already relocated to another home in another town, but had left behind part of her stuff and her two cats. The concierge took care of the cats on a regular basis, but on this particular day the cleaning woman had been in and the cats ran out. Her client begged her to go to the house and make sure the cats made their way back inside, and clean up any dead animals they may have hunted and killed during their escape. Fortunately, no animals were harmed in the story.

○ *Deliver a tube of toothpaste, 35 miles away.* One concierge works for several dental offices. One office was out of a specialty prescription toothpaste, but located one at another office. The concierge made a 70-mile-roundtrip to pick up and deliver the toothpaste as a patient waited in the office.

○ *A list of every Pizza Hut and In-N-Out Burgers between Los Angeles and Coronado, California.* A member of the Saudi Arabian royal family wanted one concierge to find out.

○ *A used golf-green mower.* The client wanted to turn his backyard into a putting green. This one took some time, the concierge said.

Sure, as Long as It's Legal, cont.

○ *A favorite laundry detergent from Puerto Rico.* A client on the East Coast wanted to have it shipped over.

○ *A rare, authentic 1882 Standard Oil Co. stock certificate signed by John D. Rockefeller.* As long as a client has the money to back up the request, almost anything may be obtained. And this item was.

○ *A place where the Moscow Circus could bathe a bear.* A concierge located an outdoor fountain and got permission for the bear to take a bath.

○ *The University of Alabama Marching Band.* A client requested this for a husband's birthday.

○ *A personal chef to fly to Greece.* One client needed a chef to come and cook for the duration of a family vacation. No problem.

○ *Diet Hawaiian Punch.* A client was disappointed when he learned his favorite diet Hawaiian Punch was being discontinued, so he asked his concierge to call all over the United States and buy up supplies of the punch. She was able to find enough punch to last him for a couple of months, which turned out to be perfect because the punch only had a shelf life of about three months. After that? Guess he had to find a new flavor of punch.

knew who to call—his personal concierge. "We were able to get tickets for his daughter to go to the concert, and his daughter was so happy that I can't even begin to tell you. So was the client," Cynthia says, laughing. "He's pretty popular around his house these days."

She has other stories, including some about a client who wanted 18-karat-gold fixtures and a custom-made bidet installed in her bathroom. "I'm serious," Cynthia says. "Could I make this up?" She's able to recall these incidents because she keeps a book detailing the most memorable requests she's received from clients.

Although there are humorous moments, Cynthia takes her job very seriously. "There is a definite trust factor that must be there between the client and the concierge," she says. "For instance, I had one client who recently made a $200,000 purchase based simply on my recommendation. My clients trust and respect my instincts, and I take the responsibility very seriously."

But don't think that every request gets filled. Even concierges, as much as they hate to, sometimes have to tell the client they just can't do it. "A few years ago, I had a client who called me the day before Bastille Day," says Cynthia. "He wanted me to make a reservation for him at a restaurant in the Eiffel Tower. But there was just no way it was going to happen. I tried, though. I had colleagues in France who just laughed when I called. If my client had just called me sooner, it could have worked out, but they were so booked up that it was impossible."

As we mentioned earlier, the concierges interviewed for this book were gracious and extremely willing to share their experiences. But there were some areas where they weren't willing to offer specifics. None of them wanted to give away their secrets on how they can fulfill last-minute requests or snag impossible-to-get concert tickets. One personal concierge, while claiming she wasn't worried about competition, coyly said that if she divulged her tips, every personal concierge would have the chance to elbow in on her business.

All the concierges interviewed agreed that they have sources and contacts in every area imaginable. How did they get those sources and contacts? Some of them made contacts when they worked as hotel concierges. Others networked with people in various businesses and gradually developed contacts that way. Although the concierges took separate paths, all of them played up the networking factor as a central component of their ongoing success. Many of them consider fellow concierges friends, but the competition factor still exists. They don't divulge every tidbit of information about their business when they lunch with a fellow concierge or run into them at a business function.

Filling the Bills

You might be wondering how your clients will be billed or what to charge for your time and effort. You want your clients to be satisfied, of course, but you also want to have a nice annual income from your business. You would probably like to get a

Sign on the Dotted Line

After you land each new client, there is one very important step you must take—draw up a contract. The contract spells out exactly what type of service you provide. It also covers fees, how often the client is billed, and when payment is due (usually in 30 days). The contract should also discuss who has the right to terminate the contract, how much notice is required, and any other particulars. It's always wise to have an attorney give the contract a once-over before finalizing it. The attorney may spot some red flags you didn't see. Don't think you can skip dealing with contracts. Every personal concierge we interviewed said contracts are vital. They protect you—and your clients.

tried-and-true fee schedule that you can use. But in the rapidly developing personal concierge industry, how you charge your clients is another one of those gray areas with no set-in-stone guidelines. What and how you are paid for your efforts is another area that you will have to research and design along the lines of your own preferences and ideas.

Most concierges have developed their own system of pricing their services, and they guard it like it's Fort Knox. Since they worked so hard to set up their business without a blueprint, you can bet they aren't going to give away those hard-earned secrets. But there are a few general patterns.

Most concierges charge their clients membership fees. Some memberships allow a certain number of requests each month for one annual fee. For those types of memberships, annual fees might start at around $1,000 to $1,500. Other memberships might be available for a smaller annual fee. For instance, if a client wants to use the concierge services only once or twice a year for small errands, a fee of $500 might be set up. Fees and contracts vary among concierges and clients.

> **Smart Tip** _Tip..._
>
> Come up with a standard reply that you can use in response to client requests. Although some hotel concierges use the very formal "That would be my pleasure," or "My pleasure," a personal concierge might want to come up with something a bit less formal. Tailor your "reply phrase" to the types of clients you'll be working with. Be creative and remember that a casual response style might work for some clients but not others.

Corporate clients are charged much higher fees because they require more services per month. For corporations, membership fees vary widely depending on the size of the company and how many requests each employee is allowed. Again, most concierges would not divulge exact fees, but a ballpark annual fee for a corporate client with many employees who are each allowed multiple requests each month could start at $5,000. More employees and a greater number of requests could drive the fee much higher.

It might be possible for a concierge who is just starting out to forgo annual membership fees and charge clients per request or per hour. For instance, you could agree to do some shopping for a client for $25 to $75 per hour or charge him a onetime fee that you settle on before you start. But most of the concierges we talked to prefer to charge membership fees because that way they are assured steady business (and a steadier income). Most of them prefer to fill six to eight requests from member clients each month rather than tackle one chore for someone who calls out of the blue and may never call again.

What happens to the bill when you've tried your best but are unable to meet the client's need? While every personal concierge has his or her own way of doing business, the norm seems to be that the client will not be charged the full amount. If considerable time and effort go into trying to fulfill a request, adding a partial fee may be appropriate.

Bright Idea

Call your clients at least once a week. Sometimes, just that simple phone call will jog their memory and remind them they do need your assistance after all!

It may sound a bit complicated at first, but after you decide what types of services you want to offer and what types of fees to charge for each, you can get your system up and running in no time. While there is no blueprint for this part of the concierge business, we've given you some ideas about how to structure your fees. As many personal concierges mentioned, when they started in this very new industry, nothing was in place to tell them how to charge their clients. They developed their own systems, and they came out on top. So will you!

Lots of Pencil Pushing

Let's change gears and talk about daily operations like paperwork and pencil pushing. You didn't think your new career was going to be all fun and games, did you? Yes, there are going to be times when you will have to turn your attention to paperwork. Things like operating expenses, for instance. I know, your eyes are probably already glazing over. But you'll have to pay close attention to such details if you want your new business to succeed, and if you want those checks from clients to keep rolling in. Do I have your attention?

For starters, you'll have daily, weekly, and monthly monetary concerns in your new business, as well as typical operating expenses. Keeping track of your expenses includes itemizing home office expenses, mileage (personal concierges do typically pay for their own mileage), and monies spent on goods for various clients. Sometimes a personal concierge will carry around a wish list for an established client. Concierges who have longstanding working relationships with clients might pick up items, knowing that they will be reimbursed.

Depending on what types of services a concierge provides, other expenses may include fees for car rentals, clothing, concert tickets, airline or trip expenses, and so on.

You will have another important bookkeeping chore if you structure your business based on membership fees. That chore will be to keep track of how many requests you have filled for a client each month. Most concierges

Smart Tip

Set aside a certain time of the month to devote to paperwork so it doesn't pile up. There are lots of software programs that make it easier to keep up with facts and figures. You can store files on your computer and have information at your fingertips. If you feel more secure having a file cabinet, you can go that route. Try buying brightly colored folders so it won't seem like such drudgery.

High Standards

Although Les Clefs d'Or is for hotel concierges, many personal concierges have adopted some of the organization's standards. The following practices are specific customer-service standards members of Les Clefs d'Or are expected to follow:

○ Listen to guests with an attentive ear.

○ Return all calls in a timely manner.

○ Always thank the guest if he or she remembers you in some way. Send thank-you notes whenever possible.

○ Never call guests by their first names.

○ Always maintain professional relationships with guests.

○ Never double-book restaurants for guests.

○ Tactfully decline illegal or unethical requests from guests.

○ Never promise guests anything unless you are sure you can deliver.

○ Always provide guests with written confirmations of their requests.

○ Advise guests upfront of surcharges or service fees on tickets or other requests.

○ Always tell guests if their seats at an event will be partially obstructed or in a poor location.

○ Inform guests of dress codes at restaurants.

○ Learn to evaluate guests by their manner, dress, and preferences. Remember that what might be good for one guest may be unsuitable for another.

said that, after a while, they develop a certain relationship and trust with their clients and will sometimes allow them more requests than spelled out in their contract. That sort of good-faith favor will certainly be remembered by the client when it's time to sign a new contract.

But the concierges said if a client's requests go way overboard one month, they will usually send an invoice the following month noting the extra services and requesting payment. Most said they balance their books and do their accounting activities once a month.

⚠ Beware!

Kathy S. describes the scope of her services by telling prospective clients, "My services are only limited by your imagination and the laws of the state of Indiana." Many concierges mention that they also make sure to point out the legalities involved. So, we wondered, what kinds of illegal activities were these hard-working entrepreneurs approached with? Two types of requests occurred regularly. In some cases, people thought the term "personal concierge" was some sort of code for an escort service. In other cases, people want a concierge to make a liquor store run for them. While the first would strike most people living outside Nevada as illegal, the second may cause you to pause. In most states, a person can only purchase and transport alcohol for their own private use. Even if your client is of legal drinking age, it's likely that you cannot purchase and deliver alcohol to him. Check your local laws to make sure your sticking to the letter of the law.

Pleasing the Client

In every interview for this book, two words kept popping up over and over again: customer service. How important is customer service in the personal concierge industry? Well, those two words pretty much embody what the profession is all about.

"To succeed in this business, you have to have a total customer service attitude. The customer is always right. You have to work to always make it better. So many people [just starting out] think this is just a quick way to earn a few bucks, but it's absolutely a business. You have to have passion to succeed at your own business," says Kathy S. "And," she adds, "Communication is key." Abbie agrees that strong communication is important, adding "flexibility and a willingness to get the job done no matter what" top the list.

Ida S. puts patience at the top of her list along with an "excellent understanding of customer acquisition and management, and the ability to multitask." Loreine G. suggests a few softer qualities for the successful concierges, "empathy, adaptability, persistence, and good ethics." Other traits noted by most of the concierges include being well-organized and an excellent time-manager.

6

Selling Service
Advertising and Marketing

For your business to be successful, you will need a lot more than just a good computer, fax machine, extra phone lines, and fancy file cabinets. You'll need clients. If this will be your first service-oriented business, you probably don't have a client base yet. Don't despair! In this chapter, we'll discuss ways to promote your business and attract clients. Once you get your first couple of clients and word spreads about what a great job you're doing, you'll soon have more business than you can handle.

So where do you get those first clients? Well, start off by telling everyone you can possibly think of that you have started your own personal concierge business. Your first clients might be your friends and acquaintances or those of family members, neighbors, and customers or operators of businesses you patronize.

"I just started putting the word out to people that I had previously worked with when I was a hotel concierge," says Cynthia A., the personal concierge from San Diego. "In the beginning, some of my clients were family members; others were friends of family members; and others were people I'd known while working at previous jobs."

Getting the Word Out

Letting the world know your business is up and running will bring clients your way. Start by attending some casual business functions and passing out business cards. For instance, find out when your local chamber of commerce, Rotary Club, or Toastmasters group holds meetings. Often, they hold breakfast meetings that can be good "meet and greet" opportunities. If you have the time, start your own networking group. You can hold meetings at a local restaurant or even line up a seminar room at a college or university and publish a print or e-mail newsletter to keep members informed of meeting times and dates.

Publish a Newsletter

Several concierges we spoke with created quarterly or monthly newsletters that they send to clients. You could send a hard copy via snail mail or choose an e-mail format. It's entirely up to you and ultimately, your clients, of course. Many people have had success with an e-mail newsletter delivered by services like Constant Contact. The price goes up based on how many addresses you send to, rather than how often you send information. So for 50 e-mail addresses it's free, for up to 500 addresses it's $15 and so on. So you have no investment until you have several clients to support the cost. You can include photos, seasonal reminders, and advertize new services. And they have reporting tools that let you keep track of how many clients are actually opening the newsletter.

Kathy S. sends her newsletter regularly to media outlets in her area. She always makes the topic timely reminding people to "weed out their old books or donate to charities, whatever works for the moment." She always gets a response. And the media keep her in mind when they need a spot to fill or an expert to talk about organizing, time management, or giving the perfect gift.

Preparing Your Elevator Speech

In this relatively new business, it pays to have an "elevator speech" or a 30-second spiel that you can rattle off when someone asks "what does that mean?" after you tell them you're a personal concierge. Jennifer C. gave me hers, "I run errands for people. I can take your dog for a walk, your cat to vet, the car to get the oil change, do your grocery shopping, and pick up dry cleaning. I can run down to Atlanta for you to pick something up or drop it off. If any of these things sound good to you, let me know; I'm here to help."

Kellye G. in Ft. Worth says she focuses on "Giving the Gift of Time to busy individuals so that they can focus on their quality time with family, friends, and work." Larissa E. found an obstacle when starting her new business, "I live in the heart of the Ozarks. . . Too often people don't understand what a concierge service is or does, so I've found it's easier to tell them I'm a personal assistant and they relate much better." Abbie M, relates to that idea, "I'm a personal assistant for anyone—for anyone who needs more time or needs to finish their 'to do' list."

Traditional Advertising

Put ads in the paper. A couple of the concierges we talked to had some luck with newspaper ads, while others found they had better results from listings in the Yellow Pages. If you're trying to cut costs, you might not want to spend all your money on expensive advertising. Have fliers made up and get permission to post them on bulletin boards in community centers, doctors' offices, dental clinics, or in break rooms

You Can Never Be Too Prepared

Nancy Roebkke, executive director of Profnet Inc., a company that specializes in teaching business professionals how to generate more revenue for their firms, shared a great networking nugget in a recent edition of *NAPO News,* the monthly newsletter of the National Association of Professional Organizers. "Always have a supply of business cards on you at all times," Roebkke says. "I know of a man who met a prospective client while on vacation, swimming in a hotel pool in Hawaii. He landed an account with the firm when he produced a business card (laminated, of course!) from his swimming trunks." Laughing at the image of that unusual networking exchange? That smart cookie is probably laughing all the way to the bank.

> **Smart Tip**
>
> As you collect business cards at various networking functions, jot down comments regarding the new contact on the back of the card. For instance, if you meet a marketing expert who specializes in an area that may help your business in the future, jot down his or her specialty on the back of the card for future reference. Then put all the cards in a spot where you can easily access them.

or cafeterias of large companies. The fliers route is one of the least costly, depending on how much you spend for the printing.

You can also send sales letters to potential clients. We've included a sample sales letter and a survey to send with it (see pages 68 and 69, respectively). Some of the concierges we talked to covered all the bases and sent sales letters, posted or mailed fliers, and placed ads in newspapers—while others picked one avenue and stuck with it.

Of course, there is always (gulp!) coldcalling. Nobody ever looks forward to coldcalling because of the fear of rejection. Admittedly, it's no fun calling 10 people in a row who say No to your pitch. But if you stick with it, that eleventh call could bring a Yes and lots of new business.

There are many other ways you can get the word out. You can send informational packets or brochures about your company to the human resources departments of large corporations in your area or deliver brochures to smaller offices. Most people like to put a face with a name; when sending a brochure or other type of flier to potential clients, think about including your photo somewhere on the mailer.

You might also join a mailing service and send your sales letters and other materials to people on mailing lists. Mailing lists focus on all types of demographics, and you can request any particular one you want to target. Dual-income families and successful businesspeople are two groups that are more likely to need concierge services, so keep this in mind when you're selecting mailing lists.

"My favorite marketing tip is wear a name tag. . . it invites people to talk to you. Then you are able to chat up the person and talk, talk, talk about your business. The more you talk about it, the easier it gets too. At first I was fumbling for words, but now it's easy and I don't mind asking them if there is something I could do for them to save them time and let them spend more time with their family," says Jennifer C., a Gainesville, Georgia, errand runner and owner of Warp Speed Errands.

A Catch-All Phrase

When you're thinking of ways to reach new clients, consider coming up with a phrase or a slogan that describes the services you offer. For instance, one concierge company proclaims: "Don't put off till tomorrow what you can delegate today." Another concierge came up with this one: "Let us Run—While you Have Fun," And yet another concierge tells customers: "We do it so you don't have to." Another one went with:

"Running Errands for the Running Ragged." Once you've chosen a slogan, stick with it. Use it on all of your advertising materials and maybe even on your stationery.

Spinning a Web

You'll also need to make sure you have a web site up and running. Just about every concierge interviewed said this was an invaluable tool in reaching potential clients. Most saw their client bases increase almost as soon as they launched their web sites.

Katharine G., the personal concierge based in Raleigh, North Carolina, says her web site is vital to her business. "Potential clients can find out what services we offer, where we're located, how to get in touch with us, and what we can do for them," she says. "We get feedback from all over the United States. When it comes to promoting our business, I wouldn't even think of not having a web site."

> **Tip...**
>
> **Smart Tip**
>
> One of the first things a new web site owner should do is look into search engine optimization, or SEO, in order to make sure your web site comes up when users search for things like "personal concierge" or other key phrases that are important to you. Considering hiring a service like Registereverywhere.com to get your webpage seen by your potential clients. As your business grows you can consider sponsoring results with specific search engines for a fee, guaranteeing that your site gets top placement in your customers' browsers.

Most of the concierges we talked to have web sites, although not all of them had those web sites when they launched their businesses. Without exception, the ones who later added web sites said they noticed an increase in business almost immediately. Some swapped links or exchanged banners with other sites, meaning that their web pages were promoted on other sites. But most of these concierges said they felt the greatest success came by registering their sites with search engines. After all, if nobody knows your site is there, what good is it?

Of course, the type of web site that will probably get you the most notice—and the most clients—is one that's professionally designed. But if you're short on funds, why not build your own web site? The free design tools offered by many of the hosting companies have many templates you can use to get started building a web site today. By doing it yourself, you'll save hundreds of dollars since the only cost you will incur is a small monthly fee for the web hosting service.

Dozens of services offer web site space, along with instructions geared to those new to the web site arena. You can build a site in as little as 30 minutes, and you don't even have to know HTML. Just click on a search engine and type in "web site hosting" or "web site promotion," and you'll get hundreds of choices.

Several companies say they offer "free" web space; however, this often doesn't apply if you intend to use your web site for commercial purposes. Be sure to read the

Sales Letter

Ace Concierge Service
123 Elm St., Mayberry, OH 12345
Phone: (123) 555-4567/Fax: (123) 555-4568

October 1, 200x

Ms. Tammy Timechallenged
777 Upside Down St.
Mayberry, OH 12345

Dear Ms. Timechallenged:

What would you think if someone told you they would take responsibility for all your business and personal errands each day so that you could have more time for yourself and your family? After all, when someone runs a large corporation like you do, you probably have no time for errands.

Well, there's no need to pinch yourself because we can make this dream a reality for you. My services range from the simple to the exotic. My company, Ace Concierge, was founded to help busy professionals like you.

Let me give you a couple of examples.

○ When was the last time your car was washed? Oh, I know. There just aren't enough hours in the day, right? Well, I can make arrangements to pick up your car while you are at work and have it washed, waxed, or detailed, and back to your office before you call it a day.

○ Or maybe you have been thinking about throwing a small dinner party but just don't have time to attend to the details. No problem! I can take care of everything for you.

I'd like to set up a meeting with you at your convenience to talk more in detail about all of the exciting services my company offers. In the meantime, please fill out the enclosed survey, which will give me a better idea of the types of services you might require.

I look forward to talking to you very soon. Please don't hesitate to call me with any questions. I can be reached at (123) 555-4567.

Sincerely,

Eva Errands

Eva Errands
Ace Concierge

P.S. I'm so interested in doing business with you that I'd like to extend a special offer to you. How does one free month of personal concierge services sound? I thought you'd like that! Once you get used to someone taking care of all your personal and business errands for you, I believe you will never want to go back to the way things were. Talk to you soon!

Survey to Enclose with Sales Letter

How often do you think you might use the services of a personal concierge? (Please circle your answer.)

a. Every day

b. Once a week

c. Once a month

d. Several times a month

What services most interest you?

a. Errand-type services

b. Business-related services

c. Personal services

d. A combination of the above

Which of the following statements best describes you?

a. I never have enough hours in the day to get everything done.

b. I certainly could use some help with personal errands.

c. If I had an extra pair of hands just one day a week, I could better manage my business.

d. All of the above

Terms and Conditions posted at these companies' web sites. You'll likely need to pay at least $5–$15 a month in web hosting fees. Even before you get your web site set up, you can e-mail your friends, family, and acquaintances and tell them that there is a new concierge in town.

Extra! Extra!

You might try to pitch a story about your new business to your local newspaper. But keep in mind that large papers get hundreds of pitches a week. So make it good. If your community has a weekly paper, you might start there first, since you won't have quite as much competition as at a larger daily paper. Don't give up if you don't hear back from an editor right away. Give it a couple of weeks and then phone the editor to ask if he or she received your information.

How do you know which advertising methods to use? Well, each person—and business—is different. What works for one person might not work for you. So think about your preferences, the clients you want to attract, and how much you can afford to spend on advertising. Then choose a method or two or three and get going. And once you find something that works for you, stick with it!

Let's Do Lunch

While you're thinking about ways to promote your business, remember that you can gain a lot by networking with others in your industry. Some of those benefits include:

○ Knowledge or insight about your industry

○ Advice about how to solve business problems

○ Leads on new business opportunities

○ Possible joint ventures

○ The chance to learn important new skills

○ Brainstorming sessions

○ Feedback and constructive criticism

So, how do you meet these new "lunch buddies"? There are many ways to find folks like yourself. Join business clubs and associations. Attend business expos and trade shows. Participate in online business-related forums, e-mail discussion groups, and chat rooms. Of course, there are lots of other ways to network. But to find them, you'll have to do a little networking of your own!

As far as ongoing advertising costs are concerned, some concierges said that after they established a client base, they didn't do much advertising apart from their web site. Others reported setting aside several hundred dollars per month for advertising. Experiment and see what works for you.

When it comes to promoting your new business, the list of avenues to pursue is endless. So, what are you waiting for? Hop to it. Clients are waiting.

Keep Them Coming Back for More

When you've implemented some of the advertising methods discussed, the clients should start rolling in—and that's a great feeling. But you can't stop there. Now for the hard work: keeping your clients happy so they'll remain your clients for the long haul.

Cynthia A., the San Diego personal concierge, says it is important to touch base with her clients on a regular basis, even if she knows they don't require her services that particular week. "I stay in touch with my clients quite frequently," she says. "At least weekly, and sometimes more often. I have great clients. Sometimes, they will end up calling me first. And they won't have any reason for calling; they just want to touch base. And oftentimes, just in talking, we'll find that they actually do need me to do something for them that week."

Cynthia says she has clients who would prefer that they were her only clients. "And I treat them like they are," she says. "In the beginning, I had one client who was excellent, but I think he really wanted to be my one and only client. Finally, he began to give others referrals about my service, but I think he wishes he could have remained my only client."

It's important for personal concierges to follow a few very important rules when dealing with clients:

- Always return phone calls promptly.
- Try to resolve any problem as soon as possible.
- If the client has a question, try to answer it quickly.

We've said it several times throughout this book but we really can't overemphasize this point: Customer service is crucial. Without good customer service, you won't have any clients. Don't make it hard for your clients to get in touch with you—it might cost you future business. Make sure they can reach you or leave a message by phone or voice mail, fax, or e-mail.

Who's Minding the Store?
Employees and Finances

Personal concierges who decide to keep their businesses small may never need employees, while others whose businesses take off so quickly they find themselves working seven days a week will need to hire some help. In this chapter, we'll take a look at some unique solutions to finding the right employees. We'll also give you tips for keeping your finances straight, and we'll talk about income statements, taxes, and other important details regarding cold, hard cash.

Help Wanted

One approach to hiring is to start off small by taking on a part-time assistant. This gives you the opportunity to assess the situation after a few months to see if you really need a full-time employee. If you aren't in the financial position to hire any help at all, perhaps you can recruit family members or friends to pitch in when necessary. Offer to buy them lunch sometime or do some errands for them in return.

New business owners can also turn to temp agencies when looking for employees. Or perhaps try to find a college student or intern. The trade-off? The student gets experience to put on her resume, and the business owner gets some much-needed help.

Growing Like a Weed

Cynthia A., the concierge from San Diego who started with a homebased business, saw her business grow so much so quickly that she ended up moving to an office away from home. Today, she has two partners in the business and uses the services of about 60 personal concierges who work for her as independent contractors. The independent contractors come in handy when she needs something handled in another city or state. She can simply call on her colleagues who live or work in those areas. Cynthia, who had previously worked as a hotel concierge, had all her contacts from those days and was able to use them to line up independent contractors in different cities who can work for her as she needs them.

Several concierges we talked to use independent contractors; these concierges have larger businesses and serve some out-of-town clients. They said they usually pay an hourly rate to the independent contractors; the pay scale is agreed upon by both parties ahead of time.

"You can also hire interns and stay-at-home moms," says Katharine G. in Raleigh, North Carolina. "They have the

Bright Idea

Stay-at-home moms definitely have their hands full with the job of running their homes and taking care of their families. But many of them are looking for additional sources of income. Consider hiring them to answer phones, locate hard-to-find items or collectibles for clients, and run errands during their free time (like when their children are in school). It might be a good fit for both of you!

An Untapped Gold Mine?

It is often said that senior citizens are living out their golden years. Well, Katharine G., personal concierge in Raleigh, North Carolina, believes tapping into some of those seniors' talents and wisdom would be akin to striking gold. "I believe our retired seniors are an untapped, natural resource," she says. "Some of these people have crackerjack minds and bodies but have been forced into retirement. If they are ready to retire, fine. But if they aren't, many of these seniors would make excellent employees." Does Katharine plan to hire any seniors at her growing company? She says, "You bet."

hours available that are compatible with your needs." By the time Katharine's business was about a year old, she had two full-time employees and was expecting to hire more soon. Katharine found one of her employees by advertising her openings in local newspapers and interviewing the applicants. She said she looked for someone who was good with people, had some customer service experience, was flexible, and could handle multiple tasks.

Angela L., the personal concierge in Austin, Texas, has four full-time employees. She found two of them through word of mouth, another through a temporary agency,

Student Aid

Want to hire a part-time employee but really don't have the funds to spare right now? You might want to look into hiring an unpaid intern. Get in touch with your local community colleges or universities and find out what requirements are in order.

Some colleges may stipulate a certain number of hours the intern must work each month, as well as what tasks they can and cannot do as part of their internship. Usually, the school will send you an application asking you to describe the job's responsibilities and your needs in terms of major, skill level, and other qualifications. Then the school will send you resumes of students who might work well with you. Each school has different requirements, so get busy and get the scoop.

▲

Bright Idea

Some personal concierges with employees find it helpful to hire a payroll service that will calculate and pay employee taxes on their behalf.

and the other by advertising in local newspapers. She mentioned the same type of qualifications as Katharine did, adding that she also looked for "real go-getters." Angela and the other concierges who were interviewed said that, except in the case of independent contractors, their employees worked on-site and also used their own vehicles with mileage reimbursements.

Katharine G. says it is vital that your employees be bonded and have car insurance. Bonding helps ensure that your clients are protected against losses from theft or damage done by your employees, and that the bonding company will be responsible for those losses—not you. "Also, it's very important that you have contracts for each of your employees," Katharine says. "This is something we take care of immediately anytime we bring in a new employee."

While the concierges we talked to were reluctant to give specific information on the employee contracts they use, the general elements include: how many hours the employee will typically work, what kinds of duties they will perform, what the pay rate will be, whether or not they will be paid mileage, and what types of benefits they will receive.

Talking Insurance

If you end up hiring employees, you're required to take certain steps to help protect their health and safety. You'll need to check out the workers' compensation insurance laws in your state because the laws do vary. Workers' comp essentially covers you and your employees for any injury or illness that occurs while an employee is at work. If you have several employees, you might also want to look into offering them health benefits. There are all kinds of policies out there that provide a range of coverage including medical, dental, vision, and life insurance.

Katharine did encounter one somewhat amusing detail when it came to insurance. "The personal concierge business is so new that my insurance company didn't yet have a category for us," she says. "So I got lumped in under limousine services. It's such a brand new field that there is nowhere to go but up."

Benefits

Most of the concierges we talked to, even the ones with employees, are still fairly small operations and so don't provide full benefits to their employees even though most of them hope to be able to do so in the near future. In the meantime, some of them do try to offer bonuses when they can, along with comp time and other incentives.

As one concierge mentioned, there are some unusual fringe benefits for concierge employees, such as the occasions when a grateful client might tip really well or offer some type of small gift. And employees occasionally get to attend special events if a client has to bow out at the last minute.

Watching Your Finances

Keeping an eye on the finances is one of the most important aspects of the job for any business owner. If the cash flow isn't, well, flowing, then your business will surely suffer.

You may not be one of those people who has a way with a calculator or views bookkeeping as something fun. Let's face it, many of us just aren't gifted in the math or accounting departments. But you don't have to be a financial whiz to keep up with the basic finances of your business.

> **Dollar Stretcher**
> When you're launching your business and making calls to attorneys or accountants, it doesn't hurt to ask if they have special discounts for new business owners!

If you have the extra resources, no matter how small your business is, you can hire a bookkeeper or an accountant to keep up with that end of the business. But even if you do put those matters into someone else's hands, it's still important to be aware of everything going on in your business. Take some time at least every few months to give the books a good once-over yourself. That's a good opportunity for you to spot any potential problems or catch anything that looks out of order.

Penny-Pinching Pointers

It's always important, especially in the early stages of a new business, to make every penny count. One way you can keep costs down is to ask for discounts from businesses you will be visiting often. For instance, if you're going to be using the same printer or courier service, let them know you'll be patronizing their place of business several times a week, if not more often. Ask them upfront about whether you can expect a discount. Don't be bashful! The worst thing that could happen is that they could say no. But more often than not, they will be glad for the repeat business and will be more than happy to offer you a discount.

Bright Idea

Why not create a separate file or folder for all documents pertaining to financial matters concerning your new business? This can include copies of contracts, insurance papers, etc. That way, those important papers will be at your fingertips when you need them. And, yes, the day will come when you will need them.

Your bookkeeper or accountant can also keep you apprised of which clients are paying on time and which clients seem to have forgotten about you. If a client is notoriously late or hasn't paid you in months, you should always pay him or her a courteous visit to see if there are any complaints about the service you are providing. Remember: Customer service is an all-important part of your business, and you don't want to dismiss any clients without looking into the situation first.

An Important Statement

You may not be familiar with an income statement, also called a *profit and loss statement.* It's really not that complicated, though. An income statement basically follows the collections and operating expenses of your business over a particular period of time. We've provided samples of income statements and a worksheet for you to create your own projected statements in this chapter (see pages 79 and 81, respectively).

Go ahead and spend some time on the worksheets tallying up some of your potential expenses and profits. Maybe you will find that you really have a knack for this sort of thing and will end up taking care of all of the financial details pertaining to your new business!

How Taxing

You can run, but you can't hide! No matter what type of business you own, the tax situation must be addressed. Of course, it's no fun, but it's a detail you absolutely must pay attention to. Otherwise, you could run into all kinds of tax troubles that could put

A Receipt Receptacle

You know those snazzy recipe holders or handy coupon holders that some folks always seem to have on hand? Shop around and find one just for your business receipts. Office supply stores have that sort of thing. And if you can't find just the right thing for you, you could always make a homemade receipts box. Go to a craft store, get the supplies, and decorate it yourself. Maybe it will make the monotonous chore of paperwork a little more fun. OK, maybe fun isn't the right word. But you get the idea.

a real damper on your business and even cost you money and clients. It's always better to be safe than sorry.

We've already mentioned the benefits of hiring an accountant, and that move is especially wise when it comes to your taxes. We're not going to get into lots of tax specifics here, but we do want to address the topic of deductions. When running a homebased personal concierge business, your tax deductions will be similar to just about any other homebased business. For example, you are allowed to deduct a percentage of the costs for your home office if you are using space solely as an office.

Income Statements

Here are monthly income statements for our two hypothetical personal concierge businesses.

Income Statements
For the month of October 2009

	ACE	First Class
Gross Monthly Income	$3,200	$9,000
Expenses		
Rent & utilities	N/A	$1,200
Employee payroll & benefits	N/A	$1,800
Phone service	$50	$125
Internet access	$20	$50
Web site maintenance	$50	$65
Advertising	$65	$100
Legal & accounting services	N/A	N/A
Insurance	$85	$165
Office supplies	$45	$125
Postage & delivery	$35	$115
Vehicle maintenance & mileage	$100	$175
Subscriptions & dues	$25	$50
Miscellaneous	$55	$120
Total Monthly Expenses	$530	$4,090
Net Monthly Profit	$2,670	$4,910

Some of the following are deductions you can claim when you have a homebased business, while others are deductions that can be taken wherever you hang your shingle. Your accountant can give you other particulars.

- *Auto expenses.* These expenses come into play any time you use your vehicle for business. For instance, when you go to the printer, post office, to visit a client, etc., keep a notebook in your vehicle so you can jot down your beginning and ending mileage. It will really come in handy when your accountant asks for your itemized expenses!

- *Phone expenses.* These include business-related phone calls and phone-service charges.

- *Entertainment expenses.* If you have a business lunch with a client, make note of it. If you present a seminar to a group of clients, you are allowed to claim the deductions for the cost of the seminar—provided the expenses were business-related.

- *Business supplies and equipment expenses, as long as they are used solely for business.* It's very important that you keep a log of which items were used for business and which items, if any, were for personal use. Your accountant—and more importantly, the IRS—may raise the question at a later date, and you'll want to have the answer ready.

- *Business-related travel expenses.* No, you can't deduct that trip to visit your sister who just had a baby. And sorry, you can't deduct that weekend getaway, either. Any travel deductions must be for business-related purposes, such as a seminar or some other event pertaining to your business.

- *Meals and hotel expenses.* The above advice also goes for this category. You are allowed to claim the deductions if attending a seminar, convention, or other business-related event. Unsure if you can claim a particular meal or hotel deduction? Ask your accountant!

It's also important to remember that concierges should never take deductions for expenses reimbursed by clients. Taxes are a special concern for those who have employees because there are all sorts of rules dictated by the IRS and state tax boards for employers. For personal concierges who provide only basic types of services, there should be few special tax issues. If in doubt, consult your attorney or tax expert.

You might also want an attorney to take a look at any contracts you sign with clients or employees and provide advice on other business matters as well. Early on, it's wise to establish a rapport with someone who has the expertise you will need at some point down the road.

Income Statement Worksheet

Income Statement

For the month of _____

Gross Monthly Income	$_____
Expenses	
Rent & utilities	$_____
Employee payroll & benefits	_____
Phone service	_____
Internet access	_____
Web site maintenance	_____
Advertising	_____
Legal & accounting services	_____
Insurance	_____
Office supplies	_____
Postage & delivery	_____
Vehicle maintenance & mileage	_____
Subscriptions & dues	_____
Miscellaneous	_____
Total Monthly Expenses	$_____
Net Monthly Profit	$_____

It's a Pleasure

All the personal concierges interviewed for this book agreed on one thing—now is the time to jump in! The field is wide open, and there's a need for professional, hard-working, customer service-oriented personal concierges. The demand is increasing, and someone will need to supply the service. It might as well be you!

▲

Top Ten Secrets of Success

Any good personal concierge should possess certain qualities. Here are a few of those keys to success:

1. Be flexible.
2. Have an abundance of patience.
3. Be resourceful.
4. Be well-organized.
5. Provide excellent customer service.

6. Be a good time manager.
7. Be a self-starter.
8. Be willing to network.
9. Be ready to juggle multiple projects.
10. Be honest, trustworthy, and dependable.

By reading this business guide, you've already taken the first step on the road to success. As you continue down that road, keep in mind that the definition of success varies from one personal concierge to another. For instance, a busy stay-at-home mother may consider her personal concierge business a success because working with a handful of flexible clients gives her some additional income while allowing her to be at home when she needs to be. Another concierge who caters to corporate clients may feel that success means being able to juggle 20 demanding, well-paying clients at all hours of the day or night. As with most things in life, success is in the eye of the beholder.

Any Regrets?

Most of the concierges interviewed had very few regrets about how they launched their businesses, but some would make changes if they could go back and start over. "I wish I had started it a lot sooner," says Katharine G., the concierge from Raleigh, North Carolina. "I realize now how big a demand there is going to be for these types of services."

Many of the concierges we spoke to also had a few words of advice for people considering getting into the business. Make sure you have enough money saved up to go out on your own. Larissa E. laments, "If I could change anything, I would have continued working to save enough money to last me a year instead of six months. I didn't believe what everyone else told me (or what I read in black and white) when everyone said it would take a solid year and sometimes two years to really get the business going." Abbie M. cautions, "Clients don't arrive overnight. You need to educate them first and then get them started. I think a lot of people believe that because this is such a great business idea that everyone else will realize it too and just come on board."

Kellye G. recommends, "Find your particular niche. It's hard to be everything to everyone." And Loreine G. reminds us, "If you do not genuinely like people and want them to succeed, this is not the industry for you. Remain open minded, flexible, and truly care about your clients." And Jennifer C. goes for the practical advice, "Make sure you have insurance from Day 1."

Ida S. reminds people that resources are out there now that weren't available just a few years ago. She encourages new concierges, "Don't do what I had to do to invent the way to become a successful concierge business owner. Apply to become a member of the Concierges Connection network and receive everything you need in one package to successfully launch your business."

> **Tip...**
> ## Smart Tip
> You'll probably get phone calls from people who will ask you to explain what a concierge is or to describe exactly what you do. Write a short description of your business (like your elevator speech) and keep it handy so you can launch right into a quick explanation when you get one of those calls while you're trying to juggle five other things.

You're on Your Way

The fact that you've reached the end of this book is cause for celebration because it means you're serious about your new business. So serious that you've read an entire book about it, studied worksheets, listened to the opinions of other personal concierges, and soaked up tips and advice from some experts.

Yep, you've come a long way, baby. But you still have a long way to go because now you need to begin the work required to make your business a reality—and a success. People all over your city need personal concierges. They need you. So what are you waiting for? Go make a name for yourself!

Appendix
Personal Concierge Resources

They say that you can never be rich enough or young enough. While we could argue with those premises, we do believe you can never have enough resources. Therefore, we present you with a wealth of sources to check into, check out, and harness for your own personal information blitz.

These sources are tidbits; ideas to get you started on your own research. They are by no means the only sources out there and should not be taken as the ultimate answer. We have done our research, but businesses tend to move, change, fold, and expand rapidly. As we have repeatedly stressed, do your homework. Get out and start investigating.

Associations

International Concierge and Errand Association (ICEA), 4932 Castor Ave, Philadelphia, PA 19124, www.iceaweb.org

National Association of Professional Organizers (NAPO), 4700 W. Lake Ave, Glenview, IL 60025, (847) 375-4746, Fax: (877) 734-8668, www.napo.net   *duem / positive*

National Concierge Association, P.O. Box 2860, Chicago, IL 60690-2860, (612) 317-2932, www.nationalconciergeassociation.com, e-mail: info@nationalconciergeassociation.com

▲

Books and Booklets

Concierge and Errand Quick Tips—An Information Guide to Get You Started, available online from ICEA, www.iceaweb.org

The Concierge: Key to Hospitality, McDowell Bryson and Adele Ziminski, John Wiley & Sons

How to Start and Operate an Errand Service, Robin C. Spina, Legacy Marketing

The Concierge Manual, 3rd Ed., Katharine Giovanni, New Road Publishing

Think and Grow Rich, Napoleon Hill, Contributor Ted Ciuba, 2005, Morgan James Publishing, LLC

The Tipping Point: How Little Things Can Make a Big Difference, by Malcolm Gladwell, Backbay Books

Concierge Consultants

Angel At Your Service, P.O. Box 6209, Whittier, CA 90609, (866) 413-7886 Fax: (866) 413-7886, www.angelatyourservice.bigstep.com, e-mail: info@angelatyour service.bigstep.com

Concierges Connection, 9982 Covewood Ct, Brecksville, Ohio 44141, (216) 373-0673, www.conciergesconnection.com, e-mail: info@conciergesconnection.com

Triangle Concierge, 1101 Eastleigh Ct, Apex, NC 27502, (919) 852-5500, www.triangle concierge.com, e-mail: kgiovanni@triangleconcierge.com

Concierge Networks

Concierge At Large Network, No telephone inquiries please. Submit inquiry via e-mail to careers@conciergeatlarge.com, fax to (619) 234-2587, or send to Concierge at Large Inc., 404 Camino Del Rio South, Suite 601, San Diego, CA 92108, Attention: Human Resources

Concierges Connection, 9982 Covewood Ct, Brecksville, Ohio 44141, (216) 373-0673, www.conciergesconnection.com, e-mail: info@conciergesconnection.com

Newsletters

Keynotes, National Concierge Association, P.O. Box 2860, Chicago, IL 60690-2860, (312) 782-6710, www.conciergeassoc.org

NAPO News, National Association of Professional Organizers, 4700 W Lake Ave, Glenview, IL 60025, (847) 375-4746, Fax: (877) 734-8668, www.napo.net

Triangle Times, Triangle Concierge, 1101 Eastleigh Ct, Apex, NC 27502, (919) 852-5500, www.triangleconcierge.com,

Personal Assistant Pro, (901) 850-9030 ext. 114, www.personalassistantpro.com

Online Forums

iVillage.com's message forums. Go to www.ivillage.com, then search for "errand services" or go directly to http://messageboards.ivillage.com/iv-wferrand?ice=ivl,searchmb

Errand Service @ Yahoo! Groups. Go to Yahoo.com, then choose "Groups," then type in "Errand_Services" or go directly to http://finance.groups.yahoo.com/group/errand_services/

Successful Concierge Services

Concierge At Large, 404 Camino Del Rio S, Ste 6011, San Diego, CA 92108, (800) 964-6887, (619) 234-7766, Fax: (619) 234-2587, www.concierge-at-large.com

Cowtown Concierge Services, 3424 Pelham, Ft. Worth, TX 76116, (817) 737-2665, Fax: (888) 262-5840, www.cowtownconcierge.com, e-mail: info@coowtownconcierge.com

The Errand Genie, (866) MY-GENIE, genie@errand-genie.com, http://www.errandgenie.com/

Lifestyle Elements, P.O. Box 570, Torrensville SA 5031, AUSTRALIA, +61 (0) 882 348 657, +61 (0) 407 972 694, www.lifestyleelements.com.au

Ms. Errands, Springfield, MO, (417) 224-2050, Fax: (417) 891-9802, www.mserrands.com, e-mail: info@mserrands.com

North Coast Concierge, Brecksville, OH, (440) 526-4004, Fax: (440) 526-4117, www.northcoastconcierge.com, e-mail: info@northcoastconcierge.com

The Perfect Solutions, 26690 Ray Ct, Elkhart, IN 46514, (574) 575-0079, www.theperfectsolutions.com, e-mail: info@theperfectsolutions.com

Triangle Concierge Inc., 1101 Eastleigh Ct, Apex, NC 27502, (919) 852-5500, www.triangleconcierge.com, e-mail: kgiovanni@triangleconcierge.com

Warp Speed Errands, P.O. Box 6587, Gainesville, GA 30504, (770) 654-WARP (9277), www.warpspeederrands.com or www.errandgoddess.com, e-mail: info@warpspeederrands.com

Glossary

Alternative office: office space that deviates from the norm, such as space shared with another professional or noncompeting business.

Concierge: someone in the business of fulfilling the requests of guests or clients; term evolved from the French *comte des cierges*, the *keeper of the candles*, who attended to the whims of visiting noblemen at medieval castles; today there are hotel concierges, corporate concierges, and personal concierges.

Corporate concierge: an employee hired by a corporation to serve the firm's other employees by running errands, picking up dry-cleaning, ordering dinner, etc.

Domain name: a web site or internet address. Sometimes referred to as a URL (Uniform Resource Location).

DSL: short for Digital Subscriber Line, it's a high speed internet connection that is always on. Typical connections allow users to receive data at 1.5 Mbps and send data at approximately 256 Kbps, rather than the 56Kbps of a standard dial-up connection. In most cases, you can keep a single line for both phone and DSL connection.

Elevator speech: a 30–60 second speech that outlines your business to prospective clients, media members, and anyone else interested in your endeavor.

Employee Dishonesty Bonds: a bond to protect a business owner from employees acting dishonestly during the course of their job.

Feng shui: the Chinese art of promoting a more harmonious flow of energy, or chi, in one's home or office.

Gold keys: the emblem adopted by the organization Les Clefs d'Or; a hotel concierge wearing crossed gold keys on his or her lapel is a member of Les Clefs d'Or.

Hotel concierge: an employee hired by a hotel to assist guests with needs that arise during their stay, such as making dinner reservations, arranging tours, and offering advice on shopping or sightseeing.

Les Clefs d'Or: a French term that means *keys of gold;* a 70-year-old professional organization of the top hotel concierges in the world. The web site for the USA organization (with more than 450 members in over 30 states) is http://www.lcdusa.org/.

Limited Liability Company: known commonly as LLCs, the term describes a way to structure your business that allows you to run your business while keeping your personal assets separate. Unlike sole proprietors, owners of LLCs can normally keep their house, investments, and other personal property even if their business fails.

Membership fees: charges collected by some concierges that allow clients a certain number of requests each month.

Mission statement: a statement that defines a company's goals and how it expects to achieve them.

Perks: the extras—such as concierge services, hair salons, espresso bars, and film processing—that some corporations provide for their employees.

Personal concierge: not employed by a hotel or corporation; instead, markets services directly to clients who pay for errand running, gift buying, making travel arrangements, etc.

Referral fees: payments from various companies given to concierges for directing business their way.

S-Corporation: a method to set up a small business (less than 100 shareholders) and avoid paying double taxes.

Sole Proprietorship: a business structure under which the business owner can be held personally liable for any business-related obligation.

Vendors: businesses used by concierges to provide their clients with various services, such as florists, caterers, and wedding planners.

Index

A

A day in the life of a personal concierge, 54–55
Accounting
  services, 49–50, 77–80
  software, 40–41
Advertising
  and marketing, 63–71
  business card, 65
  traditional, 65–66
Advice from successful concierges, 84–85
Angel At Your Service concierge products, 51, 88
Appendix, personal concierge resources, 87–90
Associated Concierge Experts (ACE), 26
Attorney services, 49–50, 77, 80

B

Better than a Butler, 24
Billing, 8, 58–60, 78
Birth and rapid growth of personal concierge field, 2–3

B (continued)

Books and booklets, recommended, 39, 88
Brochures, 47, 66
Business cards, 47
Business license, 30
Business structure, choosing a, 26–27
Business, running your, 16

C

Caller ID, 30, 46
Catch-all phrase, 66–67
Cellular phones and other gadgets, 46–47
Client pool
  diversity of, 7, 11, 14–15
  of individuals and small businesses or a combination of the two, 5, 15
  two-income families pressed for time, 5, 6, 7, 11–13
Clients
  anticipating their needs, 7
  contract, 58
  corporate, 12–13, 15

earning their trust, 8
identifying prospective, 12–13
most unusual requests, 56–57
newsletter, 64
pleasing your, 62
promoting your business and attracting, 63–71
retaining, 70–71
Cold calling, 66
Coldwell Banker Concierge, 14
Competition, checking out the, 16, 18–20
Computer
    and your internet access, 41–42
    choices, 37–39
    paper, 44
    printer, 43
    software, 39–41
    wireless, 38
Concierge at Large Network, 24, 89
Concierge by the Sea, 25
Concierges Connection, 5, 16, 85, 89
    online tools/services, 51
    website, 42
Connections, concierges as people with, 7, 55, 57–58
Consultants, concierge, 51, 88
Contract, client, 58
Corporate
    clients, 12–13, 15
    concierge, 4
Cowtown Concierge Service, 25, 89
Customer service, 62
    rules, 71

D

Deductions, expense, 80
Definition of concierge, 3, 4–5
Diverse backgrounds of those entering the personal concierge field, 2

E

Elevator speech, preparing your, 65
Employee compensation packages, concierge services included in, 12–13

Employees, 73–77
    benefits, 76–77
    bonded, 76
    hiring independent contractors, 74–75
    insurance, 76
    part-time assistant, 74
    senior citizens, 75
    stay-at-home moms, 74–75
    unpaid interns, 74, 75
Equipment checklist, start-up, 48
Errand and Concierge Service University, 51
Errand Genie, The, 25, 89
Errand Hopper, 24
Errand services, specializing in, 15
Expenses, deductible, 80

F

Fantasies, making your clients' come true, 55, 58
Fax machine, 44
Fees, 8–9, 58–61
Ferri Godmother, The, 24
Finances, watching your, 77–81
Fliers, 47, 65
Full relocation services in tandem with real estate firms, 14

G

Getting help, 51
Getting the word out, 64–70
Giovanni, Katharine, 20
Glossary, 91–92
Grocery shopper for busy corporate clients, 13
Growth, business, 30

H

Hectic lives, organizing, 2
History of the concierge, 3
Home services business replacing real estate business, 14
Homebased business, 29–30
Home office location worksheet, 32
Hospitality programs, university, 4
Hotel concierge, 3, 4, 5
Hours, working, 54

I

Illegal requests, 62
Income potential, 8–9, 58–61
Income statement, 78
    for two hypothetical personal
        concierge services, 79
    worksheet, 81
Incorporating, 27
Industry overview, 1–9, 83–85
Indy Errands Girls, 25
Insurance coverage, 49, 85
*International Concierge and Errand
    Association (ICEA)*, 3
Internet
    access, 41–42
    as useful tool for entrepreneurs, 5
    online networking forums, 18, 89
    (See also web site)
IRS business publications, 50
*It's About Time Concierge and Errand
    Service*, 24

J

Job satisfaction, 8, 83–85

L

Laying the groundwork, 23–33
Legal services, 49–50, 77, 80
Les Clefs d'Or
    customer-service standards, 61
    U.S. branch of, 4
Letterhead, business, 47
Licenses and permits, 30, 31
Lifestyle Elements, 24, 89
Limited liability company (LLC), 27
Location, business, 30–33

M

Mailing lists, 66
Market research, 18–20
    checklist, 19
Market, defining your, 11–21
Marketing
    materials, 43, 47, 49
    tools, 20
Mission statement, 15, 16
    worksheet, 17

Money is no obstacle, 35–51
Ms. Errands, 24, 30–31, 90

N

Name tag advertising, 66
Naming your business, 24–26
    business name worksheet, 28
    registering your fictitious (dba) name,
        26
*National Association of Professional
    Organizers* monthly newsletter, 65
National Concierge Association (NCA), 3
    definition of concierge, 3
Networking, 5, 18, 65, 66, 70, 85
Newsletter, client, 64
Newsletters, industry, 89
Newspaper advertising, 47
Newspaper story about your company as
    promotional tool, 69
Niche, finding your, 14–15, 18, 85
North Coast Concierge, 25, 90

O

Office set-up, 29–33
Operating system for concierge business
    owners, 16
Operations, daily, 53–62

P

Paperwork, 60–61
Part-time business, 20
Partnerships, 27
Perfect Solutions, The, 24, 90
Perk, concierge services as corporate, 12–13
Phone services, 30
Pricing, 8–9, 58–61
Printing services, 43–44, 47
Problem-solving skills, 6
Professional associations and networks, 5,
    18, 70, 88
Pronunciation of concierge, 2

Q

QuistAssist, 24

R

Real estate brokerage firms, networking
    and contracting with, 13–14

Recordkeeping, 60–61, 77–81
Requests, most unusual client, 56–57
Resources, 7, 51, 87–90

S

Sales letter, 66
    sample, 68
    survey, sample, 69
See Katie Run, 24
Seminars
    group, 20
    traveling, 51
Senior niche, 18
Services
    list of concierge, 21
    offered, from smorgasbord to
        specialized tasks, 5–6
Slogan, your company, 66–67
Sole proprietorship, 26–27
Standards and practices, customer-serv-
    ice, 61
Start-up, 35–51
    advertising, 47, 49
    capital, 50–51
    costs, 9, 36–37
    equipment, 36, 37–47
    equipment checklist, 48
    expenses for two hypothetical personal
        concierge services, 40
Stationery, business, 47
Success
    top ten secrets of, 84
    what it takes, 15–16
Successful concierge services, list of,
    89–90

T

Telephone equipment and features,
    45–47
Time-saving perks, 7, 8, 12
Tools, 20
Training sessions, concierge, 20
    online, 51
Traits of a successful concierge, 6, 7, 62
Trends, industry, 13–14

Triangle Concierge, Inc., 20, 25, 90
    consulting services and online tools, 51
    Masters Academy, 20

V

Van Goes, 24
Variety of tasks, enjoyment of, 8, 54–55
Voice mail, 30, 45–46

W

Warp Speed Errands, 25, 90
Web site
    company, 42, 67
    designing your, 42–43, 67
    hosting, 43, 69
    search optimization, 42, 67
Word-of-mouth advertising, 47

Y

Yellow Pages advertising, 65

Z

Zoning regulations, 30

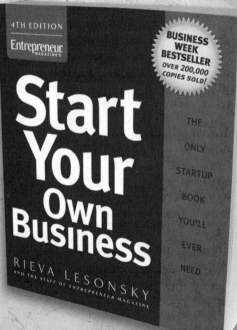

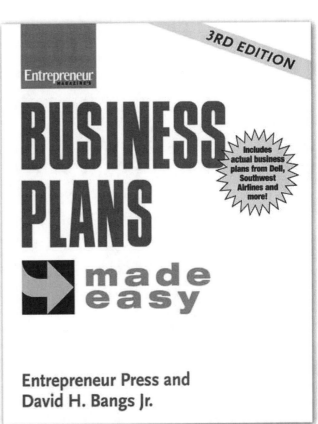